Marshes to Mansions

TREASURED RECIPES OF SOUTH LOUISIANA
JUNIOR LEAGUE OF LAKE CHARLES

Marshes to Mansions

TREASURED RECIPES OF SOUTH LOUISIANA

Published by Junior League of Lake Charles, Inc.
Copyright © 2007
Junior League of Lake Charles, Inc.
1019 Lakeshore Drive
Lake Charles, Louisiana 70601
337-436-4025 www.jllc.net

This cookbook is a collection of our favorite recipes,
which are not necessarily original recipes.

Library of Congress Number: 2007922578
ISBN: 978-0-9607524-4-7

Edited and Manufactured by **Favorite Recipes® Press**
An imprint of

FRP

P. O. Box 305142
Nashville Tennessee 37230
1-800-358-0560

Art Direction: Steve Newman and Starletta Polster
Book Design: Brad Whitfield and Susan Breining
Project Editor: Tanis Westbrook

Manufactured in China
First Printing 2007
20,000 copies

Marshes to Mansions Committee

Karen Savant Chamberlain, Chairman

Jenny Petrie Leach, Assistant Chairman

Ann Smith Todd, Sustaining Advisor

Janice Stutes Ackley

Kris Bollich Cochran

Christy Drum Ammons

Cecile Cutrer

Amber Holladay Belaire

Cassie Dingler Gage

Pam Breaux

Elizabeth Todd Martel

Kelli Abboud Wimberly

EXECUTIVE LEADERSHIP

Pam Breaux, President 2004 – 2005

Penny Ugland Seneca, President 2005 – 2006

Tracey Bleich Churchman, President 2006 – 2007

From the Photographer

I have been blessed with the ability to see the way light shapes and creates depth in an image. My passion for creating photographic art is deeply entwined with my love for the rich, colorful tapestry that is Southwest Louisiana, heaven on earth.

My lifelong experiences in the quiet forests, windswept marshes, and cypress swamps have given me a deep appreciation for the beautiful natural resources of this area. While I greatly enjoy photographing people, I am always thrilled by an opportunity to create an image of our unique blend of nature, rich heritage, and culture.

It has been my privilege to have my work showcased in such publications as *Ducks Unlimited, Good Housekeeping, Ladies Home Journal, Louisiana Life,* and *Southern Living,* and it was with great pleasure that I accepted the invitation to create the images for *Marshes to Mansions* for the Junior League of Lake Charles. This unique opportunity was exciting and challenging, particularly when pairing the familiar with the unexpected. The images selected for publication in *Marshes to Mansions* will give readers a tiny glimpse into our lives in the heart of Southwest Louisiana.

Louisianans love to cook, entertain, and enjoy life's simple pleasures. May the images and recipes in this book become a treasure to you and provide many happy memories and meals for you and your family.

Victor Monsour

VICTOR MONSOUR

Monsour's
PHOTOGRAPHY

www.monsoursphotography.com

Introduction to

Welcome to *Marshes to Mansions — Treasured Recipes of South Louisiana*. The Junior League of Lake Charles, Inc., is proud to share with you these carefully guarded family secrets, both old and new. This extensive collection of recipes, photographs, and stories is intended to present South Louisiana as it is . . . unique, in all the world!

We are excited to have *Marshes to Mansions* take you on this journey. Steeped in the traditions of Cajun, Creole, and Cowboy ancestors, yet inspired by a creative and imaginative new day, our fascinating history dictates so much of how we live. Whether we're kickin' back at the camp, serving up politics on the porch, or patiently preparing an elegant evening for family and friends, we do so in our own special way. The region's diverse natural environment colors who we are and we're delighted to share a glimpse of it with you.

As we produced this cookbook, nature compelled us to treasure people and communities like never before. On August 29, 2005, Hurricane Katrina ravaged our beloved neighbors in New Orleans and Southeast Louisiana. Cookbook production stood still as members of the Junior League of Lake Charles sprung into action, volunteering countless hours to shelter and care for displaced neighbors and friends. Before that catastrophe was over, on September 24, 2005, Hurricane Rita battered Southwest Louisiana just as cruelly. Our region was evacuated as the storm raged, and sadly the destruction it left behind was immeasurable. Thankfully, the resilience of the people was stronger than the storm and Southwest Louisiana fought back courageously. As a result, we are especially proud to showcase the Louisiana we call home.

As you explore the pages of this book, they will reveal recipes that warm hearts and homes. You'll discover The Toast of Lake Charles through appetizers and beverages. A journey Around the Lake will give you savory soups, salads, and breads. Be sure to meet us at the Cultural Crossroads for incredible entrées. Naturally, you'll want to sample the Blend of the Bayous, featuring the finest seafood and game dishes. And don't forget to add a little spice to your life with Southern Sides. Finally, The Sweet Life presents desserts that will ensure a grand finale.

Marshes to Mansions is designed to provide an unforgettable and scrumptious visit to South Louisiana. From casual to extravagant, or traditional to cutting edge, we are sure the bounties of your journey will delight you, your family, and friends.

Table of Contents

✓ Denotes recipes that may be prepared in advance

TOAST OF LAKE CHARLES
Appetizers & Beverages

In Southwest Louisiana, celebrations are our *joie de vivre*!

Community-wide festivals and fairs dot calendars almost weekly.

Yet we don't wait for special occasions to "pass a good time"

as family and friends provide ample opportunities to celebrate special

milestones or simply a new day. We crave these moments to gather

together, and frankly, we create them almost as naturally as breathing.

Join in the celebration with us as *Marshes to Mansions* begins

the way many South Louisiana occasions do, with awesome

appetizers and brilliant beverages. As you explore this chapter,

you'll discover the cuisine that makes our area so distinct.

No matter the occasion, you'll find incredible recipes that will

make you the toast of *your* town!

Appetizers & Beverages

Crawfish Beignets with Two Sauces 11 • Smoked Salmon Cocktail Sandwiches 12

Sesame Shrimp Toast 12 • Corn Crepes Filled with Barbecued Wild Duck 13

Sausage Won Ton Cups 14 • Mushroom Delights 14 • Italian Bruschetta 15

Almond-Stuffed Dates with Bacon 16 • Parmesan Puffs 16 • Creamy Blue Cheese Mushrooms 17

Smoked Gouda- and Apple-Stuffed Mushrooms 17 • Company Crab Rémoulade 18

South-of-the-Border Seafood 19 • Warm Your Heart Oyster Cocktail 19

Oyster Lettuce Rollups with Curry Sauce 20 • Oysters en Brochette 20

Bronzed Shrimp en Brochette 21 • "Grown-Up" Chicken Tenders 24 • Turkey Mushroom Pâté 25

Brie—Two Ways! 26 • Nutty and Fruity Brie 26 • Egg and Olive Spread 27

Spicy Olive Nut Spread 27 • Cool as a Cucumber Dip 27 • Presto Pesto Dip 28

Lynchburg Lemonade 28 • Berry Good Margaritas 29 • Blue Bayou Berry Margaritas 29

Cuban Mint Julep (Mojito) 30 • Key Lime Pie Martini 30 • Grand Green Apple Martini 30

Classic Lemon Drop Martini 31 • Pomegranate Martini 31 • Razzamartini 31 • Perfectly Peachie 32

Authentic Orange Sangria 32 • Creamy Coffee Punch 32 • Hot Toddie 33 • Cajun Juice 33

Pirates' Punch 34 • Wassail Punch 34 • Unexpected Eggnog 35 • Fantastic Fruit Smoothie 35

CRAWFISH BEIGNETS WITH TWO SAUCES

MAKES 16

PEPPER SAUCE
4 teaspoons peanut oil
4 roasted red bell peppers,
peeled and seeded
8 teaspoons minced onion
4 garlic cloves, chopped
Juice of 1 lemon
1 1/2 cups chicken stock
1 1/2 cups heavy cream
4 teaspoons thyme
1 teaspoon oregano
Salt and pepper to taste

MUSTARD SAUCE
4 teaspoons peanut oil
1/2 cup Dijon mustard

1 cup whipping cream
4 teaspoons balsamic vinegar

BEIGNETS
3 cups all-purpose flour
2 tablespoons cornstarch
2 teaspoons cream of tartar
1/2 teaspoon cayenne pepper
1 teaspoon salt
2 eggs
6 to 12 ounces beer made with
rice (such as Budweiser)
2 egg whites
1 pound crawfish tails
4 cups (1 quart) peanut oil

PEPPER SAUCE

Combine the peanut oil, roasted bell peppers, onion and garlic in a saucepan.
Stir in the lemon juice, stock and cream. Season with the thyme, oregano,
salt and pepper and mix well. Cook over medium-high heat until the liquid is
reduced by one-half. Purée the mixture in a blender or food processor and
return to the saucepan; keep warm until ready to serve.

MUSTARD SAUCE

Mix the peanut oil, Dijon mustard, cream and vinegar in a saucepan. Cook until
heated through; keep warm until ready to serve.

BEIGNETS

Mix the flour, cornstarch, cream of tartar, cayenne pepper and salt in a mixing
bowl. Add the eggs and enough of the beer to make a smooth batter. Beat the
egg whites in a mixing bowl until stiff peaks form. Fold into the batter. Stir in
the crawfish tails

   Heat the peanut oil to 365 degrees in a large deep skillet. Drop the crawfish
mixture by tablespoonfuls into the oil and cook for 3 minutes on each side,
turning once.

   Spoon the mustard sauce onto serving plates and place a beignet on each
plate; top with the pepper sauce.

MARDI GRAS

Glamour, mystique, beauty, and plenty of fun . . . you'll find it all during Mardi Gras in Southwest Louisiana. The celebration in the Lake Charles area began in 1882, when Momus, King of Mardi Gras, landed his royal yacht at the foot of Pujo Street and rode through the city in a chariot. Regrettably, with the onset of World War I, the celebration went underground for many years and was almost forgotten by later generations. Fortunately, those wanting to keep the tradition alive staged the first Mardi Gras Ball in Southwest Louisiana in 1964.

Today there are forty-one krewes, whose members are chosen by invitation. These organizations host balls and select members of their group to serve as royalty throughout the nearly two-month carnival season.

continued . . .

SMOKED SALMON COCKTAIL SANDWICHES
MAKES 24

12 slices white sandwich bread
1/2 cup (1 stick) butter, softened
8 ounces sliced smoked salmon
1 to 2 tablespoons finely chopped scallions,
white portion only
1 to 2 tablespoons capers
1 tablespoon grated lemon zest
6 thin slices fontina cheese

Trim the crust from the bread and butter one side of each slice. Layer the smoked salmon on the unbuttered sides of half the bread slices. Sprinkle evenly with the scallions, capers and lemon zest. Top with the cheese and the remaining bread slices, buttered side up. Arrange the sandwiches in a nonstick skillet over medium heat. Cook until the cheese melts and the bread is light brown on both sides. Cut each sandwich into four triangles and serve immediately.

SESAME SHRIMP TOAST
SERVES 4

1 tablespoon vegetable oil
2 ounces pork, finely chopped
8 fresh large shrimp, peeled, deveined and chopped
2 large garlic cloves, crushed
1 egg white
2 tablespoons sesame seeds
2 tablespoons chopped fresh cilantro
1/4 teaspoon chili powder
1/4 teaspoon white pepper
4 thick slices bread

Heat the oil in a skillet and add the pork. Sauté just until the pork is cooked through. Add the shrimp and garlic and sauté until the shrimp turn pink. Let stand for 5 minutes. Combine the mixture with the egg white, sesame seeds, cilantro, chili powder and white pepper in a bowl and mix well.

Cut the bread into circles 2 inches in diameter. Toast lightly on both sides. Spoon the shrimp mixture onto the bread rounds, pressing lightly to form a mound on each. Arrange on a broiler pan and broil just until crisp and brown on top.

CORN CREPES FILLED WITH BARBECUED WILD DUCK

SERVES 16

BARBECUED WILD DUCK
1 small red onion, chopped
2 garlic cloves, chopped
3 tablespoons unsalted butter
7 plum tomatoes, coarsely chopped
1/4 cup ketchup
2 tablespoons Dijon mustard
1 tablespoon Worcestershire sauce
2 tablespoons dark brown sugar
1 tablespoon honey
1 teaspoon chili powder
1 tablespoon chipotle chili powder
1 tablespoon paprika
1/2 teaspoon cayenne pepper
3 or 4 large wild ducks,
cleaned and patted dry
3 cups chicken stock
2 tablespoons chopped fresh cilantro
Salt and freshly ground black pepper

HABANERO SAUCE
3 cups chicken stock
1/4 cup apple juice
3 tablespoons dark brown sugar
2 star anise
1 cinnamon stick
1 habanero chile
1 tablespoon fennel seeds, toasted
Salt and pepper to taste

CORN CREPES
1/2 cup yellow cornmeal
1/2 cup all-purpose flour
1 teaspoon baking powder
Pinch of salt
1 egg
1 1/2 cups milk
1 tablespoon honey
1 tablespoon melted unsalted butter
Vegetable oil

BARBECUED WILD DUCK
Sauté the onion and garlic in the butter in a large sauté pan over medium heat until tender. Add the tomatoes and simmer for 15 minutes. Add the ketchup, Dijon mustard, Worcestershire sauce, brown sugar, honey, chili powder, chipotle chili powder, paprika and cayenne pepper; mix well. Simmer for 20 minutes. Let stand until cool and purée in a food processor.

Brush the ducks with the sauce and place in a roasting pan. Add the stock. Roast in a preheated 300-degree oven for 3 hours or until very tender and cooked through. Shred, discarding the skin and bones. Combine with the cilantro and 1/4 to 1/2 cup of the sauce in a saucepan. Season with salt and black pepper. Cook until heated through.

HABANERO SAUCE
Combine the stock, apple juice, brown sugar, star anise, cinnamon stick, chile and fennel seeds in a saucepan; mix well. Cook over medium heat until reduced to 1 cup. Strain and season with salt and pepper.

CORN CREPES
Combine the cornmeal, flour, baking powder and salt in a bowl. Mix the egg, milk, honey and melted butter in a bowl. Add to the cornmeal mixture and mix well. Heat a griddle or cast-iron skillet over medium-high heat and coat lightly with vegetable oil. Drop enough batter onto the griddle at a time to make a 5-inch crepe. Cook until light brown on both sides. Stack the crepes on a plate and cover with foil to keep warm. Mound the duck on the centers of the crepes and fold the crepes like tacos. Place on serving plates and drizzle with the habanero sauce.

Mardi Gras begins on Twelfth Night, January 6, and ends at midnight on Fat Tuesday. Street and boat parades, dances, and chicken runs are just a few of the many festivities that take place during the grand finale of the long carnival weekend. The colorful history and pageantry of this celebration is beautifully presented in the Central School Arts and Humanities building as the largest Mardi Gras Museum in the state.

Fat Tuesday is the last day of revelry and is historically the day to cook all perishable food items for a feast at winter's end. Carnival, loosely translated as "farewell to flesh," is followed by Ash Wednesday, thus marking the beginning of the forty-seven day Lenten season (forty days of Lent and seven Sundays) leading up to Easter.

SAUSAGE WON TON CUPS

MAKES 48

1 pound hot bulk pork sausage
1 1/2 cups (6 ounces) shredded Cheddar cheese
1 1/2 cups (6 ounces) shredded Monterey Jack cheese
1/2 cup ranch-style salad dressing
1/3 cup chopped pimento-stuffed olives
1/3 cup finely chopped red bell pepper
1 jalapeño chile, seeded and minced
1 (16-ounce) package 3 1/2-inch won ton wrappers

Brown the sausage in a large skillet over medium heat, stirring until crumbly; drain on paper towels. Mix with the Cheddar cheese, Monterey Jack cheese, salad dressing, olives, red bell pepper and jalapeño chile in a bowl.

Spray forty-eight miniature muffin cups with nonstick cooking spray. Place one won ton wrapper in each muffin cup, pressing to form a fluted cup. Spray the wrappers lightly with nonstick cooking spray. Bake in a preheated 350-degree oven for 8 minutes, turning the pans after 4 minutes to bake evenly.

Spoon 1 heaping tablespoonful of the sausage filling into each won ton cup. Bake for 9 to 10 minutes or until heated through and brown. Remove from the muffin cups and serve hot.

MUSHROOM DELIGHTS

MAKES 48

48 slices white bread
1/2 cup (1 stick) butter, melted
1/2 cup chopped green onions
1/2 cup (1 stick) butter
16 ounces fresh mushrooms, finely chopped
2 tablespoons all-purpose flour
1 cup whipping cream
1 tablespoon chopped parsley (optional)
2 tablespoons chopped chives
2 teaspoons lemon juice
1/2 teaspoon salt
1/4 teaspoon cayenne pepper

Cut the bread slices into rounds with a 2-inch cookie cutter. Brush with the melted butter and press in forty-eight miniature muffin cups. Bake in a preheated 350-degree oven for 10 to 15 minutes or until light brown.

Sauté the green onions in 1/2 cup butter in a skillet for 4 minutes or until tender. Add the mushrooms and sauté for 10 to 15 minutes or until tender. Remove from the heat and sprinkle with the flour, stirring to mix well. Stir in the cream gradually until smooth. Add the parsley, chives, lemon juice, salt and cayenne pepper. Cook until thickened, stirring frequently. Spoon into the toasted cups. Bake for 10 to 15 minutes or until brown and heated through.

ITALIAN BRUSCHETTA
SERVES 8

4 Roma tomatoes
Leaves of 1 large bunch basil, chopped
2 garlic cloves, crushed
3/4 cup good-quality olive oil
1 to 2 tablespoons kosher salt
1 baguette
1/3 cup mayonnaise
1/3 cup grated Parmesan cheese

Peel and chop the tomatoes, discarding the juice and seeds. Combine with the basil, garlic, olive oil and kosher salt in a bowl and mix well.

Cut the baguette diagonally into medium-thin slices. Mix the mayonnaise and Parmesan cheese in a bowl. Spread the mixture on the baguette slices. Place on a baking sheet and bake in a preheated 250-degree oven for 15 minutes. Top with the tomato mixture and serve.

Baguette
Crispy long narrow loaf of French bread

ALMOND-STUFFED DATES WITH BACON

MAKES 60

1 (4-ounce) package whole almonds
1 (16-ounce) package pitted dates
1 1/4 pounds sliced lean bacon, cut into thirds

Combine unblanched almonds with just enough boiling water to cover in a bowl. Let stand for just 1 minute; the almonds will lose their crispness if left longer. Drain, rinse under cold water and drain again. Pat the almonds dry and slip off the skins.

Place one almond in each date and wrap each with a piece of the bacon. Place on a foil-lined baking sheet. Bake in a preheated 400-degree oven for 12 to 15 minutes or until the bacon is crisp. Drain on paper towels and serve warm.

You may quick-freeze these before baking and bake frozen until the bacon is crisp, using only as many as needed. You may use almonds which have been already blanched and save that step as well.

 Make ahead

When freezing almond-stuffed dates, place the dates on a baking sheet and let them get solid. You can then transfer the items to a plastic freezer bag and they won't stick together. This will also work with fruit, cookie dough balls, and other individual items.

PARMESAN PUFFS

MAKES 36

8 ounces cream cheese, softened
1 1/2 teaspoons grated onion
2 1/2 tablespoons chopped green onions
1/2 cup (2 ounces) freshly grated Parmesan cheese
1/2 cup mayonnaise
Tabasco sauce to taste (optional)
1/4 teaspoon cayenne pepper
1 loaf thinly sliced white bread

Combine the cream cheese, grated onion, green onions, mayonnaise, Parmesan cheese, Tabasco sauce and cayenne pepper in a bowl and mix well. Chill for 30 minutes.

Cut the bread into rounds with a 1 1/2-inch cutter. Mound the cream cheese mixture onto the rounds and place on an ungreased baking sheet. Freeze until firm. Bake the frozen rounds in a preheated 350-degree oven for 15 minutes or until the topping is puffed and the bottoms are slightly crisp.

 Make ahead

CREAMY BLUE CHEESE MUSHROOMS
MAKES 20

1/2 cup chopped pecans
8 ounces cream cheese, softened
1/2 cup crumbled blue cheese
1/4 cup minced parsley
2 teaspoons Worcestershire sauce

Salt and pepper to taste
20 mushroom caps, stems removed
Olive oil
20 pecan halves

Spread the chopped pecans on a baking sheet and toast in a preheated 325-degree oven just until they begin to brown, watching to prevent overbrowning.

Combine the cream cheese and blue cheese in a bowl and beat until smooth. Stir in the chopped pecans, parsley, Worcestershire sauce, salt and pepper. Brush the outsides of the mushrooms with olive oil. Spoon a rounded teaspoon of the cream cheese mixture into each mushroom cap and top each with a pecan half. Place on a baking sheet and bake in a preheated 350-degree oven for 15 to 20 minutes or until heated through. Serve hot.

Chop a whole bunch of parsley— it freezes great! You'll have that tablespoon of fresh parsley whenever you need it.

SMOKED GOUDA- AND APPLE-STUFFED MUSHROOMS
MAKES ABOUT 30

2 pounds very large mushrooms
(about 30)
1/4 cup finely chopped onion
1 garlic clove, minced
2 tablespoons butter or margarine
2 cups (8 ounces) shredded
smoked Gouda cheese
1/4 cup bread crumbs

1 Granny Smith apple, cored
and chopped
1/4 teaspoon salt
1/4 teaspoon freshly ground pepper
3 tablespoons ground pecans
1 tablespoon butter or
margarine, melted

Remove and chop the mushrooms stems. Set the mushroom caps aside. Sauté the chopped mushroom stems, onion and garlic in 2 tablespoons butter in a skillet for 3 to 5 minutes or until tender. Remove from the heat and stir in the cheese, bread crumbs, apple, salt and pepper. Spoon evenly into the mushroom caps and place on a rack in a broiler pan. Mix the pecans and melted butter in a bowl. Sprinkle evenly over the filled mushrooms. Bake in a preheated 350-degree oven for 15 to 17 minutes or until heated through. Place under the broiler and broil for 1 to 2 minutes or until light brown on top.

Before using your cheese grater, spray it with nonstick cooking spray. That makes cleanup a breeze! The cheese washes right off without any scrubbing.

COMPANY CRAB RÉMOULADE
SERVES 4

$2/3$ cup mayonnaise
$1/3$ cup heavy cream
2 green onions, finely chopped
2 tablespoons finely chopped chives
2 teaspoons finely chopped parsley
2 tablespoons Creole mustard
1 tablespoon horseradish
2 tablespoons lemon juice
1 tablespoon white wine
$1/8$ teaspoon white pepper, or to taste
$1/8$ teaspoon cayenne pepper, or to taste
1 pound lump crab meat, shells removed and flaked
Lettuce leaves, lemon slices, parsley sprigs and
cherry tomatoes for garnish

Combine the mayonnaise, cream, green onions, chives, parsley, Creole mustard, horseradish, lemon juice, white wine, white pepper and cayenne pepper in a bowl and mix well. Add enough of the sauce to the crab meat in a bowl to coat, stirring gently. Adjust the seasonings to taste. Chill until cold. Serve garnished with lettuce leaves, lemon slices, parsley springs and cherry tomatoes.

Rémoulade

A spicy Creole mustard and mayonnaise
based sauce, often served over shrimp or other seafood

SOUTH-OF-THE-BORDER SEAFOOD

SERVES 4 TO 6

1 3/4 cups chilled clamato juice
1/3 cup bottle clam juice
1/4 cup ketchup
1/4 cup fresh lime juice
1 to 2 teaspoons Tabasco sauce
1 1/2 teaspoons salt, or to taste

1/2 cup finely chopped white onion
1/4 cup chopped fresh cilantro
2 Haas avocados, cut into chunks
8 to 12 ounces fresh jumbo lump
   crab meat
1/2 cup cooked small shrimp

Combine the clamato juice, clam juice, ketchup, lime juice, Tabasco sauce, salt, onion and cilantro in a bowl and mix well. Fold in the avocados, crab meat and shrimp gently. Chill briefly before serving.

WARM YOUR HEART OYSTER COCKTAIL

SERVES 8 TO 10

1/2 cup (1 stick) butter
2 cups cocktail sauce or chili sauce
1/4 cup Worcestershire sauce
2 cups ketchup
1 tablespoon grated lemon zest
2 tablespoons fresh lemon juice

1 cup finely chopped parsley
2 cups finely chopped celery
Tabasco sauce to taste
2 quarts oysters, cleaned
   and drained

Melt the butter in a large saucepan. Stir in the cocktail sauce, Worcestershire sauce, ketchup, lemon zest, lemon juice, parsley, celery and Tabasco sauce. Bring to a boil and reduce the heat. Simmer for 5 minutes. Add the oysters and cook for 3 to 4 minutes or until the edges curl; do not overcook. Serve with saltine crackers.

   You may make the sauce ahead of time and chill until ready to use. Heat until very hot before adding the oysters.

DOWNTOWN AT
SUNDOWN

When springtime arrives in Southwest Louisiana, the bell tolls at 5 o'clock on Fridays for the annual festivity, Downtown at Sundown. The corner of Ryan and Broad Streets takes on a new life, as live music sets the course for the weekend. Local artists, musicians, and avid dancers join downtown merchants for a South Louisiana street party. The beats of rock 'n' roll, zydeco, and Cajun draw downtown workers away from their desks and out into the streets for an evening of merriment.

Oyster Lettuce Rollups with Curry Sauce

Serves 12

12 large romaine leaves, trimmed
1 dozen plump oysters with their liquor, muscles removed
4 scallions, minced
1/2 cup (1 stick) butter
1/2 cup dry vermouth
1 cup heavy cream
1/2 teaspoon salt
1/2 teaspoon hot curry powder
3 tablespoons fresh lime juice
White pepper to taste
12 oven-baked toast points

Blanch the romaine in a saucepan of boiling water for 1 minute. Plunge the leaves into ice water to cool. Remove to paper towels to drain and pat dry. Simmer the oysters with their liquor gently in a saucepan until the edges curl; do not boil. Remove to paper towels to drain and pat dry. Place one oyster on each romaine leaf. Fold over the sides of the leaf and roll up. Arrange in a baking dish, seam side down. Sauté the scallions in the butter in a skillet for 2 minutes. Stir in the vermouth and bring to a boil. Cook until the liquid is reduced by one-half. Whisk in the cream, 1/2 teaspoon salt and curry powder. Cook for 5 minutes or until thickened. Whisk in the lime juice and season with salt and pepper. Pour evenly over the oysters. Bake in a preheated 350-degree oven until heated through. Serve each oyster with a toast point.

Oysters en Brochette

Serves 6

10 slices bacon, cut into 1-inch pieces
36 oysters
All-purpose flour for dredging
Creole seasoning
10 2/3 tablespoons (2/3 cup) butter
1/3 cup olive oil
1 1/2 teaspoons lemon juice, or to taste
1 tablespoon finely chopped fresh parsley
Lemon wedges for garnish
Toast points for garnish

Cook the bacon in a large skillet until almost done. Remove the bacon to paper towels to drain and remove the bacon drippings from the skillet. Alternate the bacon pieces with oysters on six skewers. Season flour with Creole seasoning. Dredge the skewers in the flour. Add the butter and olive oil to the skillet and heat until hot. Add the skewers and sauté until the edges of the oysters curl. Remove to a wire rack to drain and keep warm. Add the lemon juice and parsley to the pan drippings in the skillet. Cook until heated through, scraping any brown bits from the bottom of the pan. Spoon a small amount of the parsley sauce onto serving plates and top with a skewer. Garnish with lemon wedges and toast points and serve immediately.

To make toast points, trim the crusts from bread slices and butter both sides. Sauté in a skillet until light brown on both sides. Remove to paper towels to drain.

HERITAGE FESTIVAL

The annual Black Heritage Festival, usually held on the first weekend in March, continues the tradition of fostering pride and increasing cultural awareness of the legacy of the black community among residents and visitors to Southwest Louisiana. Festival activities at the Lake Charles Civic Center include gospel, zydeco, and R&B music, visual arts exhibits, pageants, contests, cheer and dance competitions, performing arts, a marketplace, and a kids' zone.

BRONZED SHRIMP EN BROCHETTE
SERVES 4

6 slices bacon
24 fresh jumbo shrimp,
peeled and deveined
2 1/2 teaspoons salt
2 teaspoons sweet paprika
1 teaspoon each garlic powder,
onion powder and
dried oregano

1 teaspoon black pepper
1/2 teaspoon cayenne pepper
1/2 teaspoon white pepper
1/2 teaspoon dried thyme
1/4 cup (1/2 stick) butter, melted
1 teaspoon butter, melted
2 teaspoons butter, melted

Blanch the bacon in a saucepan of boiling water for 2 to 4 minutes. Drain and cut into 2 inch pieces. Skewer one shrimp onto two skewers, 1 to 1 1/2 inches apart. Add one piece of bacon to the skewers. Alternate shrimp and bacon to fill four sets of skewers, using all of the shrimp and bacon.

Combine the salt, paprika, garlic powder, onion powder, oregano, black pepper, cayenne pepper, white pepper and thyme in a bowl and mix well. Pour 1/4 cup melted butter into a shallow dish. Coat each skewer in the melted butter and sprinkle with the seasoning mixture. Heat a large cast-iron skillet over high heat until very hot and beginning to smoke.

Place the skewers in the hot skillet and carefully drizzle 1 teaspoon melted butter over the skewers. Cook for 1 to 2 minutes or until the bottoms appear charred. Turn over the skewers and drizzle with 2 teaspoons melted butter. Cook for 2 minutes or until the shrimp turn pink. Serve immediately.

En Brochette

Simply means skewered, a method of cooking
usually reserved for oysters with thick
chunks of bacon in between

"Grown-Up" Chicken Tenders

Serves 10 to 12

Courir

Courir is the French word that literally means "to run." In rural Southwest Louisiana, it is used as a noun to describe a Mardi Gras run—an event that primarily takes place on Fat Tuesday. On this day large groups of masked and costumed revelers on horseback go from house to house begging for food items to be used in a communal gumbo.

Marinated Chicken Tenders
1/4 cup virgin olive oil
1/4 cup fresh lemon juice
2 garlic cloves, minced
1 teaspoon minced fresh oregano
Salt to taste
Crushed red pepper to taste
1 pound chicken tenders, trimmed
1/4 cup (1/2 stick) butter

Cucumber Sauce
1 cup sour cream
1 cup mayonnaise
Salt and pepper to taste
Lemon juice to taste
Dill weed to taste
1 cup finely chopped cucumber
1/2 cup finely chopped onion

Chicken Tenders
Whisk the olive oil, lemon juice, garlic and oregano in a bowl. Season with salt and red pepper. Pour over the chicken in a dish. Chill, covered, for 4 to 8 hours. Remove the chicken and discard the marinade. Melt the butter in a skillet. Add the chicken and sauté just until the chicken is cooked through. Adjust the seasonings to taste and serve warm.

Cucumber Sauce
Mix the sour cream and mayonnaise in a bowl. Season with salt, pepper, lemon juice and dill weed. Fold in the cucumber and onion. Serve as a dip for the chicken tenders.

TURKEY MUSHROOM PÂTÉ

SERVES 25 TO 30

1 cup chopped mushrooms
1 tablespoon butter or margarine
2 garlic cloves
12 ounces smoked turkey or boneless turkey breast,
cut into 1-inch pieces
1 1/2 cups pecans, chopped and toasted
3/4 cup mayonnaise or salad dressing
1/2 teaspoon salt
1/4 to 1/2 teaspoon cayenne pepper
1/2 cup minced green onions
2 tablespoons soy sauce
1 (17-ounce) package frozen puff pastry, thawed
Cranberry conserve (optional)

Sauté the mushrooms in the butter in a skillet over medium heat until tender and the liquid evaporates. Remove from the heat. Add the garlic to a food processor with the motor running and process for 10 seconds. Add the turkey and process for 20 seconds. Add the pecans and process for 20 seconds. Remove the mixture to a bowl. Add the mushroom mixture, mayonnaise, salt, cayenne pepper, green onions and soy sauce and mix well. Spoon into two 4 1/2×8 1/2-inch loaf pans lined with plastic wrap. Cover and chill for 8 hours.

Unfold one pastry sheet on a floured work surface and roll out to a 12×14-inch rectangle. Unmold one loaf and place it on the center of the pastry. Moisten the edges of the pastry with water and fold the ends and sides over the loaf and press the edges to seal. Repeat with the remaining pastry and loaf. Arrange seam side down on a lightly greased baking sheet. Bake in a preheated 400-degree oven for 20 minutes or until golden brown. Cut into slices and serve warm or at room temperature with cranberry conserve.

BRIE—TWO WAYS!

SERVES 6 TO 8

1 (16-ounce) round Brie cheese

OPTION 1
1/4 cup chopped red bell pepper
1/4 cup chopped green onions
1/2 jalapeño chile, chopped
1 tablespoon butter, cut into small pieces

OPTION 2
1/2 cup toasted pecans, chopped
2 tablespoons brown sugar
1/4 cup Kahlúa

OPTION 1
Remove the top rind from the cheese and discard. Sprinkle the top with the bell pepper, green onions and jalapeño chile. Dot the top with the butter. Place on a baking sheet. Bake in a preheated 350-degree oven for 10 to 15 minutes. Serve with crackers.

OPTION 2
Remove the top rind from the cheese and discard. Sprinkle the top of the brie with the pecans and brown sugar. Drizzle the Kahlúa over the top. Place on a baking sheet. Bake in a preheated 350-degree oven for 10 to 15 minutes. Serve with crackers.

NUTTY AND FRUITY BRIE

SERVES 6 TO 8

1 (13-ounce) round Brie cheese
1 (7-ounce) package mixed dried fruit, chopped
2 green onions, finely chopped
1 (2 1/2-ounce) package chopped walnuts or almonds
1/4 cup honey

Remove the rind from the cheese and discard. Place the cheese on the center of a microwave-safe plate. Combine the dried fruit, green onions, walnuts and honey in a saucepan. Cook over medium heat for 3 to 4 minutes, stirring constantly. Spoon over the cheese. Microwave on High until the cheese begins to melt and spread. Let cool slightly and serve with crackers.
  Dried cranberries and oranges are a wonderful combination.

EGG AND OLIVE SPREAD
SERVES 6

6 hard-cooked eggs
24 pimento-stuffed olives, sliced

½ cup mayonnaise, or to taste
Salt and pepper to taste

Chop the eggs coarsely. Combine the eggs, olives and mayonnaise in a bowl. Season with salt and pepper and mix well. Chill, covered, for at least 2 hours or up to 2 days. Serve on buttered bread slices.

 Make ahead

Rinse hot, hard-cooked eggs in cold water...they'll peel easier.

SPICY OLIVE NUT SPREAD
SERVES 16

1 (5-ounce) jar green olives
8 ounces cream cheese, softened
½ teaspoon black pepper
½ teaspoon cayenne pepper

½ cup mayonnaise
½ cup chopped pecans
1 to 2 white, French or sourdough baguettes

Drain the olives and chop, reserving 1 tablespoon brine. Beat the cream cheese and 1 tablespoon olive brine in a mixing bowl. Beat in the black pepper and cayenne pepper. Beat in the mayonnaise. Beat in the pecans and olives. Adjust the seasonings to taste. Chill, covered, for up to 1 week. Let stand at room temperature for a few minutes before serving. Slice the baguette and spread with the olive mixture.

Make ahead

Want to know if an egg is fresh? Place egg in a bowl of cool, salted water—if it sinks, it's fresh—if it rises to the top, throw it away!

COOL AS A CUCUMBER DIP
SERVES 16

8 ounces cream cheese, softened
1 cup mayonnaise
¾ cup sour cream
1 tablespoon Worcestershire sauce
1 tablespoon dill weed

¼ cup chopped green onions
Salt and pepper to taste
3 to 4 cucumbers, peeled, seeded and chopped

Combine the cream cheese, mayonnaise, sour cream, Worcestershire sauce, dill weed and green onions in a bowl and mix well. Season with salt and pepper. Fold in the cucumbers. Chill, covered, for 1 day before serving.

Make ahead

PRESTO PESTO DIP

SERVES 24

TAILGATING

A celebration in a parking lot with trucks backed up and their tailgates lowered to serve as an entertaining area, tailgating is the art of the pregame party. Portable grills abound as tailgaters spend hours before the ballgame preparing savory feasts, while their friends and family revel in anticipation of a win for the home team. In Southwest Louisiana the tastes of tailgating include traditional favorites like hot grilled sausages, boudin, barbecue, and spicy jambalaya. The tailgating way of life adds excitement to thousands of social calendars each fall.

1/2 cup (1 stick) unsalted butter, softened
8 ounces cream cheese, softened
8 ounces traditional feta cheese
2 garlic cloves, pressed

1/4 teaspoon pepper
1 (8-ounce) jar oil-pack sun-dried tomatoes, drained and finely chopped
1 cup basil pesto
6 ounces pine nuts

Combine the butter, cream cheese, feta cheese, garlic and pepper in a bowl and mix well with a fork. Spread equal portions of the cheese mixture into three 3 1/4×5 3/4-inch loaf pans lined with plastic wrap. Top each with a thin layer of the tomatoes. Spread the pesto over the tomatoes and sprinkle with the pine nuts. Cover with plastic wrap and chill until firm or freeze for later use. Unmold onto a serving platter and remove the plastic wrap. Serve with wheat crackers or pita chips.

 Make ahead

LYNCHBURG LEMONADE

SERVES 7

1 cup Jack Daniel's® Tennessee whiskey
1 cup Triple Sec

1 cup liquid sweet and sour mix
4 cups lemon-lime soda
Lemon slices (optional)

Combine the whiskey, Triple Sec, sweet and sour mix, soda and lemon slices in a pitcher and stir well. Serve over ice.

You may combine all ingredients except the soda in a pitcher ahead of time and keep chilled. Add the soda just before serving. This recipe can easily be doubled or tripled.

Make ahead

BERRY GOOD MARGARITAS
SERVES 24

2 (12-ounce) cans frozen
limeade concentrate, thawed
2 (12-ounce) cans frozen cranberry
juice cocktail concentrate, thawed
1 (750-milliliter) bottle tequila
1 1/2 cups Triple Sec

1 (12-ounce) bag frozen
raspberries
1 (12-ounce) bag frozen
strawberries
12 cups water

Combine the limeade concentrate, cranberry juice cocktail concentrate, tequila, Triple Sec, raspberries, strawberries and water in a large sealable freezer-safe container and mix well. Freeze until slushy. Spoon into glasses or process with ice in a blender.

Make ahead

BLUE BAYOU BERRY MARGARITAS
SERVES 4

2 1/2 cups crushed ice
1/3 cup tequila
1/4 cup Grand Marnier
1/4 cup confectioners' sugar

1 cup fresh or frozen blueberries
1 (6-ounce) can frozen
limeade concentrate

Combine the ice, tequila, Grand Marnier, confectioners' sugar, blueberries and limeade concentrate in a blender container. Process until smooth. Pour into glasses, straining if desired.

Hooch

*Illegal or cheaply produced liquor; the name
came from Hoochinoo, a tribe of Alaskan Indians
who made and sold illegal spirits*

CUBAN MINT JULEP (MOJITO)

SERVES 1

1 tablespoon sugar	1/4 cup light rum
2 mint sprigs	Juice of 1/2 fresh lime
Crushed ice	Club soda

Combine the sugar, mint and a spoonful of ice in the bottom of a glass. Crush with a spoon to release the mint flavor. Fill the glass with crushed ice. Add the rum and lime juice. Add club soda to fill the glass and stir.

You may rim the glass with "mojito" sugar crystals, if desired.

KEY LIME PIE MARTINI

SERVES 1

Graham cracker crumbs	2 tablespoons pineapple juice
1/4 cup vanilla-flavored vodka	2 tablespoons half-and-half
3 tablespoons Key lime pie syrup	1 teaspoon fresh lime juice

Coat the rim of a chilled martini glass in graham cracker crumbs. Add the vodka, Key lime pie syrup, pineapple juice, half-and-half and lime juice to a cocktail shaker filled halfway with crushed ice. Shake vigorously to mix well. Strain into the prepared glass and serve immediately.

GRAND GREEN APPLE MARTINI

SERVES 1

5 tablespoons Sour Apple Pucker schnapps, chilled	1 1/2 teaspoons Grand Marnier, chilled
2 tablespoons high-quality vodka, chilled	Crushed ice
1 tablespoon lemonade, chilled	Slice of green apple or maraschino cherry for garnish

Add the schnapps, vodka, lemonade and Grand Marnier to crushed ice in a cocktail shaker. Shake vigorously to mix well. Strain into a chilled martini glass and garnish with an apple slice.

A muddler or "mashing stick" is a wooden rod with a flat end that is used to mash or crush fruits or herbs in a cocktail. They are commonly used to get the oil and full flavor from mint leaves for a mint julep or mojito, limes for caipirinhas, or cherries for old-fashioneds. They are also a great tool for crushing garlic, spices, or nuts on a board, or as a pestle in a bowl.

Keep vodka in the freezer. It won't freeze solid and it will keep your cocktail cold longer without melting the ice.

CLASSIC LEMON DROP MARTINI

SERVES 1

Lemon wedge	2 tablespoons lemonade, chilled
Sugar	2¹/₂ tablespoons Cointreau, chilled
3 tablespoons citrus-flavored	1 teaspoon simple syrup, chilled
vodka, chilled	Maraschino cherry for garnish

Dampen the rim of a chilled martini glass with the lemon wedge and dip the rim in sugar to coat. Add the vodka, lemonade, Cointreau and simple syrup to crushed ice in a cocktail shaker. Shake vigorously to mix well. Strain into the prepared glass. Garnish with a cherry and serve immediately.

POMEGRANATE MARTINI

SERVES 1

¹/₄ cup pomegranate juice	Squeeze of fresh lemon juice
2 tablespoons vodka	Splash of sparkling water
1 tablespoon Cointreau	Pomegranate seeds or strip of
1 teaspoon simple syrup	lemon peel for garnish

Combine the pomegranate juice, vodka, Cointreau, simple syrup and lemon juice with crushed ice in a cocktail shaker. Shake vigorously to mix well. Add the sparkling water and stir gently. Strain into a martini glass and garnish with pomegranate seeds or lemon peel. Serve immediately.

RAZZAMARTINI

SERVES 1

2 tablespoons vodka	¹/₄ cup lemon-lime soda
2 tablespoons	Strip of lemon or lime peel
raspberry-flavored liqueur	for garnish
1 tablespoon lemonade	

Add the vodka, raspberry-flavored liqueur and lemonade to crushed ice in a cocktail shaker. Shake vigorously to mix well. Add the soda and stir gently. Strain the liquid into a martini glass and garnish with the lemon peel. Serve immediately.

Simple syrup is very easy to make and is used in many cocktails to add volume and sweetness. Measure equal amounts of sugar and water. Bring the water to a boil in a saucepan. Add the sugar and cook until the sugar is dissolved, stirring constantly. Once the sugar is dissolved completely, remove the pan from the heat. Allow to cool completely and bottle. Flavored syrups may also be made by simply adding such spices as cardamon, ginger, and vanilla beans.

PERFECTLY PEACHIE

SERVES 4

3 whole canned peaches in juice or 3 fresh peaches, peeled and pitted	1 (6-ounce) can frozen pink lemonade concentrate
³/₄ cup vodka	8 cups cracked ice

Process the peaches, vodka and lemonade concentrate in a blender until
smooth. Add the ice and process to mix well. Pour into stemmed glasses
and serve. You may make this ahead and freeze in a sealable freezer-safe
container. Let stand at room temperature for 30 minutes before serving.

Make ahead

AUTHENTIC ORANGE SANGRIA

SERVES 6 TO 8

¹/₂ orange	¹/₂ cup Triple Sec or
¹/₄ cup sugar	Cointreau
2 cups orange juice	Juice of 1 lime
1 (750-milliliter) bottle red wine	¹/₂ orange, sliced

Remove the peel from the ¹/₂ orange and place the peel in a bowl. Add the
sugar and mash with a fork to release the orange flavor. Combine the orange
juice, red wine, Triple Sec and lime juice in a bowl and mix well. Add to the
sugar mix and stir to mix well. Let stand for 15 minutes. Remove and discard
the orange peel. Pour the sangria into a pitcher and add the orange slices.
Serve over ice.

CREAMY COFFEE PUNCH

SERVES 25 TO 30

6 cups hot brewed coffee	1 cup Kahlúa (optional)
2 cups milk	1 quart vanilla ice cream
¹/₂ cup sugar	1 quart coffee ice cream
1 tablespoon vanilla extract	

Combine the coffee, milk, sugar and vanilla in a bowl and stir until the sugar is
dissolved. Chill until cold. Pour the mixture into a punch bowl. Add the Kahlúa
and mix well. Scoop the vanilla ice cream and coffee ice cream into the punch.
You may make this punch without the Kahlúa for a nonalcoholic version.

HOT TODDIE
SERVES 20

2 cups (4 sticks) butter, softened
1 (1-pound) package dark brown sugar
1 quart vanilla ice cream, softened
Rum (optional)
Boiling water
Cinnamon sticks

Beat the butter and brown sugar in a mixing bowl until light and fluffy.
Add the ice cream and mix well. Freeze in a sealable freezer-safe container.
Add 1 heaping tablespoon of the frozen mixture to a mug. Add 2 to
3 tablespoons rum. Add boiling water to fill the mug and stir with a cinnamon
stick. Repeat to make additional servings.
    If making without the rum, use 2 tablespoons of the frozen mixture.

*For a blackberry spritzer, thread
fresh blackberries on a 6-inch
wooden skewer. Freeze 1 hour.
Dip the rim of a glass in corn
syrup, and roll in grated lime
zest (about 1 lime). Place frozen
blackberry skewer in prepared
glass. Pour chilled sparking
water over skewer, and garnish
with a mint sprig. These skewers
are also beautiful in lemonade,
iced tea, or any flavored fruit juice.*

CAJUN JUICE
SERVES 30

2 cups water
6 regular tea bags
1 cup sugar
1 (6-ounce) can frozen limeade concentrate
1 (6-ounce) can frozen pink lemonade concentrate
Mint leaves for garnish

Bring the water to a boil in a saucepan. Remove from the heat and add the
tea bags. Let steep, covered, for 10 to 15 minutes. Remove the tea bags and
add the sugar. Stir until the sugar is dissolved. Pour into a 4-quart pitcher.
Add the limeade and lemonade concentrates and stir until melted. Add enough
cold water to make 2 quarts. Add ice to fill the pitcher. Serve garnished
with mint leaves.

*Faced with the coming heat, what
goes down easier than cool, icy
water? Water flavored with the
irresistible tang of blackberries.
We found out that you can turn
blackberries into luscious ice cubes
that will flavor a glass of water
as they thaw. Try it to create a
refreshing drink that looks—and
tastes—like the essence of summer.*

PIRATES' PUNCH

SERVES 30 TO 35

2 cups water   1 cup water
1 1/2 cups sugar   1 (1 1/4-ounce) bottle
2 (12-ounce) cans frozen lemonade   almond extract
concentrate, thawed   2 (2-liter) bottles ginger ale
2 (46-ounce) cans pineapple juice

Combine 2 cups water and sugar in a saucepan. Cook until the sugar dissolves, stirring frequently. Remove from the heat and let cool. Combine the sugar mixture, lemonade concentrate, pineapple juice, 1 cup water and almond extract in a bowl and mix well. Pour into a sealable freezer-safe container or sealable plastic freezer bags and freeze until firm. Let stand at room temperature for 1 to 2 hours. Remove to a large bowl. Add the ginger ale and stir until slushy.

Make ahead

WASSAIL PUNCH

SERVES 25

1 gallon apple juice   1 cup sugar
1 quart orange juice   24 whole cloves
1 quart pineapple juice   4 cinnamon sticks
1 cup bottled lemon juice

Combine the apple juice, orange juice, pineapple juice, lemon juice, sugar, cloves and cinnamon sticks in a saucepan. Simmer for 10 minutes or until hot and the sugar is dissolved, stirring frequently.

Soirée

A dance party

UNEXPECTED EGGNOG

SERVES 8

1 (12-ounce) can frozen grape-raspberry
juice cocktail concentrate, thawed
1 (1 quart) carton eggnog, chilled
1 (12-ounce) can lemon-lime soda, chilled
Whipped cream and ground nutmeg for garnish

Combine the grape-raspberry juice cocktail concentrate and eggnog in
a pitcher and stir well. Add the soda and stir carefully. Pour into glasses and
dollop with whipped cream and sprinkle with nutmeg.

FANTASTIC FRUIT SMOOTHIE

SERVES 2

8 ounces frozen strawberries, thawed
1 large banana
6 ounces strawberry yogurt
1 (15-ounce) can sliced peaches in heavy syrup, chilled
1 cup small ice cubes
Whipped cream and maraschino cherries for garnish

Combine the strawberries, banana, yogurt, peaches and ice cubes in a blender
and proccss until smooth. Pour into glasscs and garnish with whipped cream
and maraschino cherries.

Most frozen fruits and canned fruits work well in this recipe.

CONTRABAND DAYS

Contraband Days, a twelve-day festival extravaganza filled with savory Cajun food, family fun, and activities, is attended by more than 200,000 people annually. Each year, during the first two weeks in May, the city officially celebrates the legend of the pirate Jean Lafitte. History tells us that Lafitte and his band of pirates once sailed the area's waterways and are said to have buried contraband treasure somewhere in the vicinity of the lake, quite possibly Contraband Bayou, hence the name. The event is kicked off every year with a pirate ship bombardment to "take control of the city" at the seawall of the Lake Charles Civic Center. A gang of rowdy and unruly buccaneers, led by Jean Lafitte himself, overruns the blazing cannons of the local militia and raises the "Jolly Roger" flag as they capture the Mayor and force him, with swords drawn, to walk the plank into the swirling waters of the lake. Thus begins two weeks of pageantry and festivities. Contraband Days is one of the largest festivals in Louisiana, second in size only to the New Orleans' Mardi Gras. In addition to the Contraband Days, our area is host to more than seventy-five other festivals and has been nicknamed The Festival Capital of Louisiana.

AROUND THE LAKE
Soups, Salads & Breads

The early settlers of Lake Charles came from Bordeaux, France,
and lived peacefully with several Native American tribes already
here in the area. Over the years, these two tradition-based cultures
formed a new and unique community that continues today.

We can thank our ancestors for our love of the outdoors and strong
ties to the numerous waterways that flow through the region.
These lakes and bayous are vital to both work and play. We love few
things more than enjoying a meal on or beside the water.

In this chapter, we present you with a selection of our finest soups,
salads, and breads. Your travels through theses pages will reveal favorite
Creole comforts — delicious dishes to begin your repast.

Soups, Salads & Breads

Louisiana Bouillabaisse 39 · Crabby Bisque 40 · Lagniappe Crawfish Soup 41

Creamy Crawfish Soup 42 · Sunday Oyster Stew 42 · Oyster Artichoke Truffle Soup 43

Real Deal Shrimp and Oyster Gumbo 44 · Duck and Sausage Gumbo 45

Contraband Bayou Turtle Soup 46 · Spanish Sauce (for Turtle Soup) 47 · Cream of Brie Soup 47

Hearty Vegetable Soup 48 · Roasted Red Pepper Soup 49 · Rustic Tomato Bisque 49

"It's About Thyme" Soup 50 · Cold Tomato and Crab Soup 50 · Chilled Cucumber Soup 51

Strawberry Soup 51 · Balsamic Pear Salad 54 · Chutney Salad 54 · Orange Marmalade Salad 55

Raspberry Chipotle Salad 55 · Red, White and Blue Spinach Salad 56

Watermelon and Cucumber Salad 56 · Bistro Salad with Warm Goat Cheese 57

Mock Caesar Salad 57 · Muffuletta Salad 58 · Nutty Broccoli Slaw 58 · Uptown Tomatoes 59

Barbecue Chicken Salad 59 · Cran-Raspberry Chicken Salad 60 · Blue Cheese Dressing 60

Parmesan Dressing 61 · Croutons 61 · Basic Beer Bread 61 · Spiced Pumpkin Bread 62

Broccoli Corn Bread 62 · Confetti French Bread 63 · "Oh So Good" Cheese Biscuits 63

Cornmeal Sage Biscuits with Sausage Gravy 64

Southern Sweet Potato Biscuits 64 · Do-Ahead Bran Muffins 65 · Cinnamon Brunch Bread 65

Grand Marnier French Toast 66 · Old-Fashioned Pancakes 67

LOUISIANA BOUILLABAISSE

SERVES 6 TO 8

1/2 cup olive oil
2 garlic cloves, minced
3/4 cup chopped onion
2 carrots, sliced
1 (16-ounce) can tomatoes
1/2 teaspoon crumbled saffron
1/2 teaspoon bottled dried
 orange peel
1/2 teaspoon fennel seeds
1/2 teaspoon dried thyme
2 tablespoons minced parsley
1/2 cup dry red wine

1 (6-ounce) can tomato juice
4 (8-ounce) bottles clam juice
Salt and freshly ground pepper
 to taste
Tabasco sauce to taste
1 pound fresh deveined
 peeled shrimp
1 (1-pound) container crab fingers
1 quart oysters, cleaned and
 cut in half if large
Hot cooked rice (optional)

Heat the olive oil in a large saucepan. Add the garlic, onion and carrots and sauté for 5 minutes. Add the tomatoes, saffron, orange peel, fennel seeds, thyme and parsley and sauté for 2 minutes. Stir in the wine, tomato juice and clam juice. Simmer for 30 minutes. Season with salt, pepper and Tabasco sauce. Add the shrimp and cook until they turn pink. Add the crab and cook until heated through. Bring to a boil. Add the oysters and cook until the edges curl; do not overcook. Serve immediately with French bread and a green salad or serve the soup over hot cooked rice.

You may freeze this soup before adding the shrimp, crab and oysters. Complete the soup when ready to serve.

Louisiana Bouillabaisse

A Louisiana version of a classic Provençal recipe

CRABBY BISQUE

SERVES 12 TO 16

1 cup (2 sticks) butter
Kernels from 8 ears fresh corn (3 cups)
1 cup chopped onion
1 cup chopped celery
$1/2$ cup chopped red bell pepper
$1/4$ cup chopped garlic
1 cup all-purpose flour
10 cups seafood stock or chicken stock
2 cups heavy whipping cream
$1/2$ cup sliced green onions
$1/2$ cup chopped parsley
1 pound jumbo lump crab meat
Salt and white pepper to taste
Tabasco sauce to taste

Melt the butter in a 2-gallon stockpot over medium-high heat. Add the corn, onion, celery, bell pepper and garlic and sauté for 5 to 10 minutes or until the vegetables are tender. Whisk in the flour and cook until a white roux forms, whisking constantly; do not let brown. Add the stock, one ladle at a time, stirring constantly. Bring to a gentle boil and reduce the heat. Simmer for 30 minutes, stirring occasionally. Add the cream, green onions and parsley. Cook for 3 minutes, stirring frequently. Fold in the crab meat gently, being careful not to break the lumps. Season with salt, white pepper and Tabasco sauce.

You can simmer the corncobs with water to make a corn stock. Cook until the liquid is reduced to 4 cups. Use the corn stock in place of 4 cups of the seafood stock.

Tabasco

Means "damp earth," the Tabasco pepper is combined with vinegar and salt to make a sauce sold throughout the world by the McIlhenny family.

Lagniappe Crawfish Soup

Serves 12 to 16

5 pounds boiled whole crawfish
1 gallon boiling water
3 large onions, chopped
2 bell peppers, chopped
1 bunch parsley chopped
3 to 4 tablespoons vegetable oil
2 cups (4 sticks) butter
1 cup all-purpose flour
1 tablespoon Cajun seafood seasoning
Kernels from 8 ears cooked corn
2 pounds cooked small potatoes, chopped
2 cups whipping cream
1 cup chopped green onions

Peel the crawfish and reserve the meat. Combine the crawfish heads and shells with the boiling water in a stockpot. Boil for 20 minutes. Strain the stock into a container and discard the heads and shells. Reserve 10 cups of stock in a large saucepan and freeze the remaining stock for later use.

Sauté the onions, bell peppers and parsley in the oil in a saucepan until tender. Add the butter and cook until the butter is melted. Add the flour and cook for a few minutes, stirring constantly. Add the reserved crawfish meat and Cajun seasoning. Cook for 5 minutes, stirring constantly. Heat the reserved crawfish stock to boiling. Stir in the crawfish mixture. Boil for 5 minutes, stirring occasionally. Add the corn and potatoes. Cook for 2 minutes. Remove from the heat and stir in the cream and green onions.

You may use one 16-ounce carton of chopped seasoning instead of the onion, bell pepper and parsley. Refer to sidebar for options.

You can boil your own crawfish, potatoes, and corn together and proceed with the recipe or you can buy all of them from a seafood store already boiled. If you boil garlic with it, save the garlic and add pieces to the bowl for anyone that wants it.

Wrap celery, onions, green onions, etc. in foil and place in the refrigerator to keep crisp.

CREAMY CRAWFISH SOUP
SERVES 6 TO 8

1 pound crawfish tails   1/2 bunch green onions, chopped
1/2 cup chopped onion   4 cups half-and-half
1 cup (2 sticks) butter   2 teaspoons garlic powder
1/2 cup all-purpose flour   2 teaspoons onion powder
2 cups chicken broth   1 to 2 teaspoons cayenne pepper

Grind the crawfish in a food processor and set aside. Sauté the onions in the butter in a saucepan until tender. Stir in the flour and cook for 2 minutes, stirring constantly. Stir in the broth and simmer for 5 minutes, stirring frequently. Stir in the crawfish and green onions. Simmer for 5 minutes, stirring constantly. Stir in the half-and-half and simmer for 5 minutes. Stir in the garlic powder, onion powder and cayenne pepper. Simmer for 20 minutes, stirring occasionally. Remove from the heat and let stand for a few minutes before serving.

SUNDAY OYSTER STEW
SERVES 30

1 gallon oysters with their liquor   1 tablespoon black pepper
1 1/2 cups (3 sticks) unsalted butter   1 tablespoon white pepper
1 cup all-purpose flour   1 tablespoon Tabasco sauce
8 quarts half-and-half   1/2 cup (1 stick) unsalted butter,
2 tablespoons salt   cut into pieces

Drain the oysters, reserving their liquor. Cut large oysters in half. Melt 1 1/2 cups butter in a large stockpot over medium heat. Stir in the flour. Cook until the roux is light brown, stirring constantly. Stir in the reserved oyster liquor. Stir in the half-and-half. Bring to a gentle simmer, stirring frequently. Stir in the salt, black pepper, white pepper and Tabasco sauce. Add the oysters and cook until the edges curl. Adjust the seasonings to taste. Add 1/2 cup butter gently and allow it to melt on the surface of the stew.

    This recipe may easily be halved or quartered.

OYSTER ARTICHOKE TRUFFLE SOUP

SERVES 4

2 artichokes
16 oysters with their liquor
1/3 cup minced scallions
3 tablespoons butter
1 white truffle, chopped, or 1 tablespoon truffle oil
plus 8 ounces chopped mushrooms
3 tablespoons all-purpose flour
2 cups cream
Salt and white pepper to taste
Tabasco sauce to taste
1 tablespoon minced parsley

Cook the artichokes in a saucepan of boiling water for 45 minutes or until tender;
drain. Remove the bottoms and coarsely chop. Discard the leaves. Poach the
oysters in their liquor in a saucepan until the edges curl. Drain, reserving 2 cups
of the cooking liquid. Remove the muscles from the oysters and cut the oysters
in half, if large. Sauté the scallions in the butter in a saucepan just until tender.
Stir in the chopped artichoke bottoms and truffle. Add the flour and cook
for a few minutes, stirring constantly. Whisk in the reserved oyster liquid and
cream. Cook over low heat until slightly thickened, stirring frequently. Season
with salt, white pepper and Tabasco sauce. Stir in the oysters and parsley and
cook just until heated through.

Truffle
An underground fungus usually found at the
roots of oak trees whose fleshy edible fruiting
body is highly valued as a delicacy

REAL DEAL SHRIMP AND OYSTER GUMBO

SERVES 8

Shrimp shells
2 quarts water
2 ribs celery, cut into pieces
1 onion, quartered
1 cup (2 sticks) margarine
1 cup all-purpose flour
3 onions, chopped
3 ribs celery, chopped
1 green bell pepper, chopped
6 garlic cloves, minced

1 (10-ounce) bag frozen
   chopped okra
1 (10-ounce) can tomatoes with
   green chiles
1 (8-ounce) can tomato sauce
Salt and pepper to taste
Tabasco sauce to taste
2 pounds fresh deveined
   peeled shrimp
4 cups oysters
Hot cooked rice

Combine the shrimp shells, water, celery and onion in a saucepan. Bring to a boil and reduce the heat. Simmer for 20 minutes. Strain the stock into a container and discard the solids.

Melt the margarine in a heavy skillet. Stir in the flour. Cook until the roux is dark brown, stirring constantly. Add the onions, celery, bell pepper, garlic and okra. Cook over low heat for 10 minutes, stirring frequently. Stir in the tomatoes with green chiles and tomato sauce. Remove the mixture to a stockpot. Stir in the hot shrimp stock gradually. Cook, covered, over low heat for 1 1/2 hours. Season with salt, pepper and Tabasco sauce. Remove from the heat and let cool. Chill, covered, for 3 hours to overnight. Heat the gumbo over medium heat until it begins to boil. Add the shrimp and cook until they turn pink. Add the oysters and cook until the edges curl. Serve over hot cooked rice with hot French bread. Offer gumbo filé powder at the table.

Filé

Ground sassafras leaves used to thicken
and add flavor to gumbo

DUCK AND SAUSAGE GUMBO

SERVES 4 TO 6

$1/2$ cup vegetable oil	$1/4$ cup chopped green onion
4 large ducks, cleaned and patted dry	2 tablespoons chopped garlic
	2 tablespoons chopped parsley
3 quarts water	5 teaspoons salt
4 onions, chopped	1 teaspoon black pepper
6 ribs celery, chopped	$1/2$ teaspoon cayenne pepper
$1\,3/4$ cups vegetable oil	Tabasco sauce to taste
$1\,1/2$ cups all-purpose flour	Filé powder to taste
3 cups chopped onions	1 pound andouille sausage, chopped
1 cup chopped celery	
1 cup chopped bell pepper	4 cups cooked rice

Heat $1/2$ cup oil in a heavy skillet. Add the ducks and brown on all sides. Remove the ducks with a slotted spoon to a large saucepan, reserving the stock. Add the water, 4 onions and 6 ribs celery. Bring to a boil and reduce the heat. Simmer until the ducks are tender and cooked through. Remove the ducks with a slotted spoon to a work surface. Debone the ducks and cut into pieces.

Add $1\,3/4$ cups oil to the skillet. Stir in the flour. Cook over medium heat until the roux is dark brown but not burned, stirring frequently. Add 3 cups onion, 1 cup celery, the bell pepper, green onion and garlic. Cook until the onion is translucent, stirring frequently. Heat the stock to boiling. Add the flour mixture by spoonfuls and stir until dissolved.

Add the duck and reduce the heat. Stir in the parsley, salt, black pepper and cayenne pepper. Season with Tabasco sauce and filé powder. Add additional water if necessary to make the consistency of a medium thin cream soup.

Simmer for 3 hours, adjusting the seasonings to taste every hour. Skim any excess fat from the top of the gumbo. Brown the sausage in a skillet over medium heat. Remove with a slotted spoon to paper towels to drain. Stir the sausage into the gumbo and adjust the seasonings to taste. Serve over the hot rice.

A neat trick for removing excess fat from soup or gravy is to skim the surface with ice wrapped in cheesecloth. The fat congeals and clings right to the cloth.

Rice in a salt shaker will keep the dampness out.

Contraband Bayou Turtle Soup

Serves 18

Charpentier District

The downtown Charpentier (Char pah t yeah) District is a 20-block area of one of the state's finest collections of late-1800 and early-1900 restored Victorian homes. Because there were no architects in Lake Charles until the early 1900s, the homes reflect individual characteristics of the carpenters and the builders. We honor the carpenters of that time by naming our district "Charpentier," which is French for carpenter. This intriguing district was admitted to the National Register of Historic Places in 1990. It continues to attract locals and tourists alike to explore its historic streets and marvel at its distinct architectural style.

5 pounds turtle meat	6 tablespoons chopped
2 unpeeled onions	flat-leaf parsley
4 quarts water	1 teaspoon dried thyme
1/4 cup beef base	3 tablespoons whole allspice tied
1/2 cup (1 stick) butter	in cheesecloth
1 cup (2 sticks) butter	6 whole cloves
8 ounces ham, cubed	1/4 teaspoon mace
1/4 cup minced garlic	1/4 cup Worcestershire sauce
6 cups finely chopped onions	1 tablespoon sea salt, or to taste
2 cups finely chopped celery	1 tablespoon white pepper
2 cups diced tomatoes	1 tablespoon freshly ground
3 lemons	black pepper
9 cups Spanish Sauce (page 47)	1/2 cup madeira
1 cup strained vegetables from	3 hard-cooked eggs, grated
Spanish Sauce	1 cup plus 2 tablespoons sherry
6 Turkish bay leaves	

Debone the turtle meat, saving the bones. Grind or mince the meat and set aside. Arrange the bones on a rack in a broiler pan. Broil until brown on all sides. Remove the bones to a stockpot. Remove the root end from 2 onions and cut in half; do not peel. Place, cut side up, on a rack in a broiler pan. Broil until blackened. Add the onions to the stockpot. Add the water. Bring to a boil and cook for 1 hour or longer. Add the beef base and stir until dissolved. Strain the stock into a container and discard the bones and onions.

Melt 1/2 cup butter in a heavy skillet. Add the turtle meat and sauté until golden brown. Melt 1 cup butter in a stockpot. Add the ham, garlic and onions and sauté until the onions begin to brown. Add the celery and sauté until tender. Stir in the turtle meat. Cook for 15 minutes, stirring occasionally. Stir in the tomatoes. Cook for 10 minutes, stirring occasionally.

Juice the lemons and remove the seeds. Add the lemon juice to the soup. Mince the lemon peel and pulp and add to the soup. Stir in the 12 cups of the turtle stock, the Spanish Sauce, Spanish Sauce vegetables, bay leaves, parsley, thyme, allspice, cloves, mace, Worcestershire sauce, salt, white pepper and black pepper. Simmer for 2 hours, stirring occasionally. Stir in the madeira and eggs. Remove the bay leaves and allspice. Ladle into serving bowls and top each serving with 1 tablespoon sherry.

SPANISH SAUCE (FOR TURTLE SOUP)

MAKES 10 CUPS SAUCE

1/2 cup (1 stick) butter
2 1/2 cups finely chopped onions
2 1/2 cups finely chopped carrots
10 garlic cloves, minced
5 ribs celery, finely chopped
1 tablespoon dried thyme
10 Turkish bay leaves
15 sprigs flat-leaf parsley
2 tablespoons sugar
1 cup Savoie's roux
4 quarts hot chicken stock
4 cups tomato sauce

Melt the butter in a large heavy saucepan. Add the onions and carrots and sauté until most of the liquid evaporates and the vegetables are beginning to brown. Stir in the garlic, celery, thyme, bay leaves, parsley and sugar. Simmer until the garlic and celery are tender, stirring frequently. Add the roux and cook until dissolved, stirring constantly. Stir in the stock. Stir in the tomato sauce. Bring to a boil and reduce the heat. Simmer for 1 hour. Strain the sauce into a container. Reserve 1 cup of the strained vegetable mixture and discard the remainder.

CREAM OF BRIE SOUP

SERVES 4

1/2 cup chopped onion
1/2 cup chopped celery
1/4 cup (1/2 stick) butter
1/4 cup all-purpose flour
1 (14-ounce) can chicken broth
2 cups milk
1 (16-ounce) round Brie cheese, rind removed
Crumbled cooked bacon (optional)
Chopped chives for garnish

Sauté the onion and celery in the butter in a saucepan until tender. Stir in the flour. Cook for a few minutes, stirring constantly. Stir in the broth and milk. Cook for 5 minutes or until thickened, stirring constantly. Add the cheese and cook until the cheese is melted, stirring frequently. Process the soup in a blender and return to the saucepan. Stir in the bacon. Ladle into serving bowls and sprinkle with chives.

HEARTY VEGETABLE SOUP
SERVES 10

1 (2-pound) boneless beef chuck roast
1 onion, chopped
1 rib celery with leaves, chopped
Salt and pepper to taste
2 soup bones
1 (28-ounce) can diced tomatoes
4 red potatoes, cut into quarters
3 turnips, cut into quarters
1 onion, coarsely chopped
3 ribs celery, chopped
8 ounces fresh string beans, trimmed
6 carrots, sliced
1 (10-ounce) package frozen baby lima beans
1 (10-ounce) package frozen corn

Combine the roast with enough water to cover in a stockpot. Add 1 onion, 1 rib celery, salt and pepper and cook for 1 hour. Add the soup bones and cook for 1 hour or until the roast is tender. Remove the roast to a platter using a slotted spoon.

Add the tomatoes, potatoes, turnips, 1 onion, 3 ribs celery, the string beans and carrots to the broth mixture and cook until the vegetables are tender. Stir in the lima beans and corn and cook for 10 minutes longer.

Cut the roast into bite-size pieces and return to the stockpot. Cook until heated through. Remove and discard the soup bones. Adjust seasonings to taste. Ladle into soup bowls.

Liaison

A binder or thickening agent for soups and sauces;
now the term is commonly used to refer to a person
"binding" parties together

ROASTED RED PEPPER SOUP

SERVES 3 TO 4

2 large red bell peppers   Salt and pepper to taste
1 onion, chopped   1/2 cup white wine
2 tablespoons butter   1 (10-ounce) can low-sodium
4 garlic cloves, minced   chicken broth
1/2 teaspoon dried thyme   1 cup heavy cream

Cut the bell peppers in half lengthwise and remove the seeds. Place cut side down on a baking sheet. Broil until the skins are blackened. Remove the bell peppers to a bowl and cover with plastic wrap. Let stand for 5 minutes. Peel the bell peppers and discard the blackened peels. Chop the bell peppers. Sauté the onion in the butter in a saucepan over medium heat until tender. Stir in the garlic, bell peppers and thyme. Season with salt and pepper. Stir in the wine and heat to almost boiling. Reduce the heat and stir in the broth and cream. Simmer for 5 minutes. Remove from the heat and let cool slightly. Purée the soup in a blender. Return the soup to the saucepan. Cook for 5 minutes over medium heat. Serve immediately.

To intensify the flavor and maintain the nutritional value of vegetables, they should be roasted instead of boiled. Line a baking sheet with baking parchment. Put vegetable pieces on the pan, sprinkle with olive oil, and toss. Roast at 425 degrees until tender, about 10 to 15 minutes. Add salt and pepper to taste.

RUSTIC TOMATO BISQUE

SERVES 8

3 (28-ounce) cans whole tomatoes   2 teaspoons sugar
1/2 teaspoon salt   1 1/2 teaspoons salt
1/4 teaspoon white pepper   1 1/2 teaspoons white pepper
1/2 cup (1 stick) unsalted butter   1 teaspoon cracked black pepper
16 (or more) shallots, sliced   1 teaspoon cayenne pepper
1/4 teaspoon salt   1 teaspoon garlic powder
1/4 teaspoon white pepper   3 cups half-and-half

Spread the tomatoes and juice over the bottom of a 10×14-inch baking pan. Season with 1/2 teaspoon salt and 1/4 teaspoon white pepper. Bake in a preheated 350-degree oven for 45 minutes, stirring occasionally. Melt the butter in a skillet. Add the shallots, 1/4 teaspoon salt and 1/4 teaspoon white pepper and sauté until tender. Purée the tomatoes and shallots in batches in a blender and pour into a heavy 5-quart saucepan. Stir in the sugar, 1 1/2 teaspoons salt, 1 1/2 teaspoons white pepper, the black pepper, cayenne pepper, garlic powder and half-and-half and heat to almost boiling. Reduce the heat and simmer for 15 minutes, stirring frequently.

To remove the lingering smell that raw garlic leaves on your hands, wash your hands in cold water and rub them all over with table salt, then wash in soap and warm water. Repeat if necessary until the odor is gone.

"It's About Thyme" Soup
Serves 6

1 cup (2 sticks) unsalted butter
8 zucchini, cut into 1/4-inch slices
Kosher salt to taste
3 tablespoons minced garlic
2 tablespoons chopped fresh thyme
1/4 teaspoon crushed red pepper flakes
4 cups chicken broth
Shredded Parmesan cheese for garnish

Melt the butter in a large skillet over medium heat. Increase the heat to medium-high. Add the zucchini, spreading evenly over the bottom of the skillet. Season with kosher salt. Cook until the zucchini is brown, stirring occasionally. Add the garlic, thyme and red pepper flakes. Cook for 2 minutes, stirring frequently. Remove from the heat and let stand for 5 minutes. Purée the zucchini mixture in batches in a blender and pour into a saucepan. Whisk in the broth. Simmer for 5 minutes. Ladle into serving bowls and sprinkle with Parmesan cheese.

Cold Tomato and Crab Soup
Serves 4

8 ounces plain yogurt
3 cups tomato juice
1 tablespoon olive oil
1 tablespoon lemon juice
1 tablespoon red wine vinegar
1/4 small onion, finely chopped
1/2 teaspoon curry powder
1/4 teaspoon salt
3 tablespoons chopped basil
1 pound (or more) lump crab meat, shells removed

Whisk the yogurt into the tomato juice in a bowl. Whisk in the olive oil, lemon juice, vinegar, onion, curry powder, salt and basil. Adjust the seasonings to taste. Chill until cold. Ladle into serving bowls and top with crab meat.

CHILLED CUCUMBER SOUP

SERVES 6 TO 8

3 pounds cucumbers, peeled, seeded and
coarsely chopped
1 cup sour cream, well chilled
1/4 cup mild olive oil
1 teaspoon white wine vinegar
1/2 teaspoon balsamic vinegar
2 1/4 teaspoons chopped fresh dill weed
2 1/4 teaspoons sugar
1 1/2 teaspoons salt, or to taste
1 1/2 cups full-fat buttermilk
Pepper to taste
Fresh dill weed for garnish

Combine the cucumbers, sour cream, olive oil, white wine vinegar, balsamic
vinegar, dill weed, sugar and salt in a bowl and mix well. Shake the buttermilk
well before measuring and stir into the cucumber mixture. Season with pepper.
Purée the mixture in batches in a blender and pour into a large bowl. Adjust
the seasonings to taste. Chill, covered, for at least 2 hours or up to 1 day. Stir
before serving. Ladle into serving bowls and garnish with dill weed.

 Make ahead

*Use a melon baller to remove seeds
from the cucumber. Cucumber
soup may be served beautifully
in delicate demitasse cups as first
course or for a buffet.*

STRAWBERRY SOUP

SERVES 4

1 cup fresh strawberries, halved
1 cup orange juice
1/2 cup white wine
1/4 cup honey
1/4 cup sour cream
1 1/2 teaspoons tapioca instant pudding mix
1/8 teaspoon cinnamon
Fresh strawberries and sour cream for garnish

Purée the strawberries, orange juice, wine, honey, sour cream, pudding
mix and cinnamon in a blender. Pour into a microwave-safe bowl. Microwave
on High for 5 to 6 minutes and stir to mix well. Chill, covered, until cold.
Stir before serving. Ladle into serving bowls and garnish with pieces of fresh
strawberries and a dollop of sour cream.

 Make ahead

BALSAMIC PEAR SALAD

SERVES 8

2 cups pecans
6 to 8 bunches baby spinach, rinsed and patted dry
1 bunch green onions, thinly sliced
1/2 cup olive oil
1/4 cup extra-virgin olive oil
1/3 cup balsamic vinegar
Salt and freshly ground pepper to taste
3 ripe pears, cored and sliced
1 1/2 cups dried cherries

Spread the pecans on a baking sheet. Bake in a preheated 325-degree oven for 5 to 10 minutes or until starting to brown. Remove the pecans to a bowl and let cool. Combine the spinach and green onions in a large bowl. Whisk the olive oil, extra-virgin olive oil and vinegar in a bowl. Season with salt and pepper. Add 1/2 cup of the dressing to the pecans and toss to coat. Add the pecans, pears and dried cherries to the spinach mixture. Add the remaining dressing and toss to coat. Serve immediately.

CHUTNEY SALAD

SERVES 12

2 (10-ounce) packages mixed salad greens
2 avocados, chopped
2 cucumbers, peeled and sliced
1 (8- to 10-ounce) package shredded carrots
1 cup sweetened dried cranberries
1/2 cup sliced almonds, toasted
2 cups grape tomatoes, halved
1 (4-ounce) package crumbled basil and herb feta cheese
Salt and pepper to taste
1 envelope Italian salad dressing mix
1/2 cup vegetable oil
1/4 cup balsamic vinegar
3 tablespoons mango chutney or other fruit chutney
Croutons (optional)

Combine the salad greens, avocados, cucumbers, carrots, dried cranberries, almonds, tomatoes and cheese in a large bowl. Season with salt and pepper.

Whisk the salad dressing mix, oil, vinegar and chutney in a bowl. Drizzle over the salad and toss to mix. Sprinkle with croutons and serve.

ORANGE MARMALADE SALAD

SERVES 6 TO 8

MARMALADE DRESSING
1/3 cup sesame oil or other oil
1 teaspoon minced garlic
2 tablespoons minced shallots
2 tablespoons orange marmalade
1 tablespoon cider vinegar
1/2 teaspoon salt
1/2 teaspoon pepper

FRUIT AND GREENS SALAD
1 large head romaine, torn into
  bite-size pieces
1 apple or pear, cored
  and julienned
1 can mandarin oranges, drained
1 cup walnuts, almonds or
  pecans, toasted

DRESSING
Whisk the sesame oil, garlic, shallots, marmalade, vinegar, salt and pepper in
a bowl. Let stand for 30 minutes but no longer than 1 hour.

SALAD
Combine the romaine, apple and mandarin oranges in a bowl and toss to mix.
Add the dressing and toss to coat. Top with the walnuts and serve.

RASPBERRY CHIPOTLE SALAD

SERVES 6

1/4 cup raspberry chipotle sauce
1/3 cup plain fat-free yogurt
1 tablespoon Dijon mustard
2 teaspoons olive oil
1/8 teaspoon salt
1/8 teaspoon pepper
2 to 3 tablespoons water

1 (10-ounce) package mixed
  field greens
1/2 cup crumbled feta cheese
1/3 cup sweetened dried cranberries
1/2 cup glazed walnuts
2 cups fat-free restaurant-
  style croutons

Whisk the raspberry chipotle sauce, yogurt, Dijon mustard, olive oil, salt, pepper
and water in a bowl. Place the mixed greens in a large bowl. Top with the
cheese, dried cranberries, walnuts and croutons. Add the dressing and toss
to mix.

RED, WHITE AND BLUE SPINACH SALAD

SERVES 6

1 cup strawberries
1 to 2 green onions
1 teaspoon salt
3 tablespoons sugar
1/3 cup raspberry vinegar
1 cup extra-light olive oil
1 to 2 (6-ounce) packages baby spinach
1 cup strawberries, sliced
1 cup blueberries
2/3 cup crumbled blue cheese
1/2 cup chopped pecans or walnuts

Purée 1 cup strawberries, the green onions, salt, sugar, vinegar and olive oil in a blender.

Combine the spinach, 1 cup sliced strawberries, the blueberries, cheese and pecans in a large bowl and toss to mix. Add the dressing just before serving and toss to coat.

WATERMELON AND CUCUMBER SALAD

SERVES 10 TO 12

4 cucumbers, peeled, seeded and diced
1 teaspoon salt
1/4 red onion, thinly sliced
1/4 cup white vinegar
1/4 cup sugar
1/4 teaspoon crushed red pepper flakes
8 cups cubed seeded watermelon

Combine the cucumbers and salt in a bowl and toss to mix. Remove to a colander and let drain for 30 minutes. Pat the cucumbers dry with a paper towel and place in a bowl. Add the onion. Combine the vinegar, sugar and red pepper flakes in a saucepan. Bring to a boil and boil for 1 minute, stirring occasionally. Remove from the heat and let cool for 1 minute. Pour over the cucumbers and onion and toss to coat. Chill, covered, overnight. Add the watermelon just before serving and toss to mix.

CAMERON PARISH

Cameron Parish, the largest land mass in the state, was organized in 1870. The parish reportedly took its name from Simon Cameron, President Lincoln's secretary of war. The earliest inhabitants were Attakapas Indians. Recollections of early days tell of the enormous orange crops, with some trees producing five thousand oranges. Today the agriculture is centered on rice and corn.

BISTRO SALAD WITH WARM GOAT CHEESE

SERVES 4

3 tablespoons good-quality olive oil
1 tablespoon fresh lemon juice
1 large garlic clove, chopped
Salt and pepper to taste
1 (4-ounce) log fresh goat cheese

1/4 cup finely chopped pecans or walnuts, toasted
4 generous handfuls of mixed torn lettuce
1/4 cup coarsely chopped pecans or walnuts, toasted

Whisk the olive oil, lemon juice and garlic in a bowl. Season with salt and pepper. Slice the cheese into four rounds and coat with 1/4 cup finely chopped pecans, pressing the pecans into the cheese. Arrange the coated cheese rounds on an oiled baking sheet. Bake in a preheated 400-degree oven for 6 to 8 minutes. Combine the lettuce and dressing in a bowl and toss to coat. Divide the salad equally among four serving plates. Top each with a round of warm goat cheese and sprinkle with 1/4 cup coarsely chopped pecans.

MOCK CAESAR SALAD

SERVES 8

2 tablespoons lemon juice
1/4 cup fat-free sour cream
1 tablespoon Worcestershire sauce
3 tablespoons olive oil
1 to 2 tablespoons water
1 large garlic clove, minced
1/4 teaspoon freshly ground black pepper
Dash of salt

1/4 cup freshly grated Parmesan cheese
2 (10-ounce) packages chopped romaine
3 cups fat-free restaurant-style croutons
3/4 cup (3 ounces) freshly grated Parmesan cheese

Whisk the lemon juice, sour cream, Worcestershire sauce, olive oil, water, garlic, salt, pepper and 1/4 cup cheese in a bowl. Combine the romaine, croutons and 3/4 cup cheese in a large bowl. Add the dressing and toss well to coat. Serve immediately.

MUFFULETTA SALAD

SERVES 6

3 tablespoons balsamic vinegar
1 tablespoon water
2 teaspoons orange juice or lemon juice
1 teaspoon garlic juice
1/2 teaspoon cracked pepper
1/4 teaspoon sugar
1/8 teaspoon salt
1/2 cup olive oil

1 (10-ounce) package romaine hearts, or 1 head romaine, torn into bite-size pieces
1 cup broccoli slaw
3 to 4 tablespoons oven-roasted sliced almonds
3 to 4 tablespoons shredded Parmesan cheese
1/2 cup Italian salad olive mix

Whisk the vinegar, water, orange juice, garlic juice, pepper, sugar, salt and olive oil in a bowl. Combine the romaine and broccoli slaw in a bowl and toss to mix. Add the almonds and cheese and toss to mix. Add the olive mix and dressing just before serving and toss to mix.

NUTTY BROCCOLI SLAW

SERVES 12 TO 14

2 (3-ounce) packages beef ramen noodles, crumbled
3/4 cup sugar
1 cup vegetable oil
2/3 cup cider vinegar
2 (12-ounce) packages broccoli slaw
1 cup sliced almonds
1/2 cup sunflower seeds

Whisk the seasoning packets from the ramen noodles, sugar, oil and vinegar in a bowl. Combine the broccoli slaw, almonds, sunflower seeds and ramen noodles in large bowl. Add the dressing and toss to mix. Chill for 30 minutes or up to 2 days.

 Make ahead

UPTOWN TOMATOES
SERVES 4

2/3 cup extra-virgin olive oil
1/3 cup white wine vinegar
1 tablespoon Dijon mustard
2 garlic cloves, minced
1/2 teaspoon sugar
1 teaspoon salt
Freshly ground pepper to taste
8 thick slices of large tomatoes

Salt to taste
1/2 cup thinly sliced green onions, white portions only
1 cup canned artichoke hearts, coarsely chopped
2 tablespoons capers
1/2 cup parsley, finely chopped

Whisk the olive oil, vinegar, Dijon mustard, garlic, sugar and 1 teaspoon salt in a bowl. Season with pepper.

Arrange the tomatoes on a serving platter and season with salt and pepper. Sprinkle with the green onions. Top with the artichokes, capers and parsley. Drizzle the vinaigrette over the tomatoes.

Make ahead

The pickled and salted caper bud is often used as a seasoning or garnish. Capers are a common ingredient in Mediterranean food.

BARBECUE CHICKEN SALAD
SERVES 4 TO 6

4 to 6 boneless chicken breasts
1 cup barbecue sauce
1 (10-ounce) package mixed salad greens
1 tomato, diced
4 to 6 ribs celery, chopped
Chopped green onions to taste
1 (16-ounce) can whole kernel corn, drained

1 (15-ounce) can black beans, drained and rinsed
1 (8-ounce) bottle ranch salad dressing
1/2 to 3/4 cup barbecue sauce
1 (8-ounce) package shredded Cheddar cheese or Colby cheese
Crushed tortilla chips

Marinate the chicken in 1 cup barbecue sauce in a shallow dish for 30 minutes. Remove the chicken and discard the sauce. Grill the chicken until cooked through. Remove to a work surface and cut into slices. Combine the salad greens, tomato, celery and green onions in a bowl and toss to mix. Add the corn and black beans and toss to mix. Add the salad dressing and 1/2 cup barbecue sauce and toss to coat. Sprinkle with the cheese and tortilla chips. Arrange the sliced chicken over the top of the salad.

CRAN-RASPBERRY CHICKEN SALAD

SERVES 10

4 cups chopped cooked chicken
1/2 cup mayonnaise
12 ounces raspberry yogurt
1/2 cup pecans, chopped
1 (6-ounce) package sweetened dried cranberries
3 to 4 ribs celery, finely chopped
1/4 cup minced green onions

1 1/2 teaspoons lemon juice, or to taste
1 1/2 teaspoons salt, or to taste
1 1/2 teaspoons curry powder, or to taste
Cayenne pepper to taste
10 croissants or lettuce leaves

Combine the chicken, mayonnaise, yogurt, pecans, cranberries, celery, green onions, lemon juice, salt and curry powder in a bowl. Season with cayenne pepper and mix well. Spread between split croissants for sandwiches or serve over lettuce leaves.

 Make ahead

BLUE CHEESE DRESSING

MAKES 4 CUPS

16 to 24 ounces blue cheese, at room temperature
1/3 to 1/2 cup buttermilk
1/4 cup olive oil
2 tablespoons cider vinegar
Juice of 1/4 lemon
1/2 cup chopped onion

2 garlic cloves, chopped
1 teaspoon Worcestershire sauce
1/2 teaspoon Tabasco sauce
Salt to taste
1 tablespoon (or less) pepper
1 cup sour cream

Crumble the cheese into a bowl. Remove two-thirds of the cheese to a blender container. Add the buttermilk, olive oil, vinegar, lemon juice, onion, garlic, Worcestershire sauce, Tabasco sauce, salt, pepper and sour cream to the blender. Process at low speed for 30 seconds. Add to the cheese in the bowl and stir gently. Chill, covered, overnight or up to 8 days.

Make ahead

SULPHUR

Sulphur is the second largest city in Southwest Louisiana. Its name comes from the large sulphur deposit discovered in the area in the 1860s. In time, one of the world's largest sulphur industries was established there. Their local Brimstone Museum chronicles this and other interesting facets of their history. The city continues to flourish, just across the lake from Lake Charles. Other nearby communities include Westlake, Moss Bluff, DeQuincy, and Vinton.

PARMESAN DRESSING

MAKES 2 CUPS

1 cup (4 ounces) freshly grated Parmesan cheese
1 cup vegetable oil
1/4 cup red wine vinegar
2 teaspoons (or more) Dijon mustard or Creole mustard
1 teaspoon salt
1 teaspoon freshly ground pepper

Process the cheese, oil, vinegar, Dijon mustard, salt and pepper in a blender.
Serve at room temperature. Chill any leftovers in a jar with a tight-fitting
lid for up to 2 weeks. Shake well before serving.

Make ahead

BASIC BEER BREAD

SERVES 7 TO 9

3 cups self-rising flour
1/2 cup sugar
1 (12-ounce) can beer
1/4 cup (1/2 stick) butter, melted

Combine the flour, sugar and beer in a bowl and stir just until moistened.
Spoon the batter into a loaf pan coated with nonstick cooking spray. Bake in
a preheated 350-degree oven for 30 minutes. Pour the melted butter evenly
over the top of the bread. Bake for 15 minutes longer. Cool in the pan for
10 minutes. Remove to a wire rack to cool.

*To make your own croutons,
melt 1/2 cup (1 stick) of
butter on a baking sheet in
a preheated 400-degree oven.
Reduce the oven temperature to
275 degrees. Add fresh bread
cubes to the melted butter
and toss to coat. Bake until
golden brown and crisp, stirring
occasionally. Remove to a paper
towel and let stand until cool.
Store in an airtight container.*

*When you buy bread in a
grocery store, have you ever
wondered which is the freshest
so you "squeeze" for softness?
The best way to ensure you are
purchasing fresh bread is to
look at the color of the twist tie
to see what day it was delivered.
Bread is delivered five days per
week and is represented this way:
Monday = blue, Tuesday =
green, Thursday = red, Friday =
white, and Saturday = yellow.*

SPICED PUMPKIN BREAD

SERVES 24

3 1/2 cups all-purpose flour	3 cups sugar
2 teaspoons salt	1 cup vegetable oil
2 teaspoons baking soda	4 eggs, beaten
1 teaspoon baking powder	1 (16-ounce) can pumpkin
1 teaspoon each cinnamon, nutmeg and allspice	2/3 cup water
	1/2 to 1 cup chopped pecans
1/2 teaspoon cloves	Raisins (optional)

Mix the flour, salt, baking soda, baking powder, cinnamon, nutmeg, allspice and cloves together. Beat the sugar, oil and eggs in a mixing bowl until light and fluffy. Stir in the pumpkin. Stir in the dry ingredients. Add the water, pecans and raisins and mix well. Spoon the batter into two well-greased loaf pans. Bake in a preheated 350-degree oven for 1 hour or until the bread tests done. Cool in the pans for 10 minutes. Remove to a wire rack to cool.

BROCCOLI CORN BREAD

SERVES 10 TO 12

1 (10-ounce) package frozen chopped broccoli,
thawed and drained
1 onion, finely chopped
3 eggs
3/4 cup small curd cottage cheese
2 (8-ounce) packages corn muffin mix
3/4 cup (1 1/2 sticks) butter, melted

Mix the broccoli, onion, eggs, cottage cheese, corn muffin mix and butter in a bowl. Spoon the batter into a nonstick 9×13-inch baking pan. Bake in a preheated 375-degree oven for 45 minutes. Remove to a wire rack to cool.

CONFETTI FRENCH BREAD

SERVES 10 TO 12

1/2 cup (1 stick) butter, softened
1/2 cup mayonnaise
1 cup pitted black olives, chopped
2 garlic cloves, chopped
6 green onions, chopped
2 cups (8 ounces) shredded mozzarella cheese
1 large loaf French bread, cut in half horizontally

Beat the butter and mayonnaise in a bowl until light and fluffy. Add the olives, garlic, green onions and cheese and mix well. Spread over the cut sides of the bread and place on a baking sheet, cut side up. Bake in a 350-degree oven for 15 to 20 minutes or until the cheese is melted.

"OH SO GOOD" CHEESE BISCUITS

MAKES 25

2 cups self-rising flour
1/2 cup (2 ounces) shredded sharp Cheddar cheese
1/3 cup (heaping) shortening
3/4 cup milk, at room temperature
1/2 cup (1 stick) butter, melted

Combine the flour, cheese and shortening in a bowl and mix well with hands. Stir in the milk to form a dough. Turn out the dough onto a floured work surface and cut into biscuit-size pieces. Pour the melted butter into a shallow dish. Coat the dough pieces in melted butter and arrange on a nonstick baking sheet. Bake in a preheated 400-degree oven for 10 minutes.

Meunière

"Miller's wife" — a style of cooking using a light dusting of flour and sautéeing in butter

CORNMEAL SAGE BISCUITS WITH SAUSAGE GRAVY

SERVES 6

TUTEN PARK

Tuten Park, established as a city park in 1999, is located on Nelson Road in Lake Charles. It was named in honor of a community leader who contributed the forest to the city. Visitors can observe wildlife and nature while strolling along 6,000 feet of walking paths. Presently, efforts are being made to tag and identify trees, as well as develop a butterfly and hummingbird garden. Additionally, there is an ongoing effort to produce other projects that will focus on species conservation and ecological education.

SAUSAGE GRAVY
1 pound bulk pork sausage
1/4 cup all-purpose flour
2 1/4 cups milk
Salt and pepper to taste

CORNMEAL SAGE BISCUITS
1 3/4 cups baking mix
1/2 cup yellow cornmeal
1 teaspoon dried sage leaves, crumbled
2/3 cup milk

GRAVY
Brown the sausage in a skillet until cooked through. Remove to paper towels to drain and break the sausage into small pieces. Remove the drippings from the skillet and add the flour. Cook for 1 minute, stirring constantly. Add the milk and season with salt and pepper. Cook for 5 minutes or until thickened, stirring constantly. Stir in the sausage and keep warm.

BISCUITS
Combine the baking mix, cornmeal and sage in a bowl. Add the milk and stir until a soft dough forms. Beat for 30 seconds. Drop by twelve spoonfuls onto a greased baking sheet. Bake in a preheated 450-degree oven for 8 to 10 minutes or until golden brown. Serve the gravy over the biscuits.

SOUTHERN SWEET POTATO BISCUITS

MAKES 25

1 cup (heaping) mashed baked sweet potatoes
1/2 cup sugar
1/2 teaspoon vanilla extract
2/3 cup shortening
2 cups self-rising flour, sifted
1/2 cup buttermilk

Combine the sweet potatoes, sugar and vanilla in a bowl and mix well. Cut the shortening into the flour in a bowl. Add the sweet potato mixture and stir just until blended. Add the buttermilk gradually and mix just until moistened. Roll out the dough on a floured work surface and cut with a biscuit cutter. Place the biscuits on an ungreased baking sheet. Bake in a preheated 400-degree oven for 20 minutes or until light brown. Serve alone or cut in half horizontally and fill with sliced ham.

DO-AHEAD BRAN MUFFINS

MAKES 48

5 cups all-purpose flour
4 teaspoons baking soda
2 teaspoons salt
2 teaspoons cinnamon
1 teaspoon nutmeg
1 cup wheat germ (optional)
1 (15-ounce) box raisin bran cereal

4 eggs
2^1/$_2$ cups sugar, or 1^1/$_2$ cups honey
4 cups buttermilk
1 cup canola oil
1 cup applesauce, or 1 banana, mashed (optional)

Combine the flour, baking soda, salt, cinnamon, nutmeg and wheat germ in a bowl and mix well. Stir in the cereal. Beat the eggs and sugar in a large mixing bowl. Add the buttermilk and canola oil and mix well. Stir in the applesauce. Add the dry ingredients and mix well. Chill, covered, for up to 2 weeks, if desired. Fill desired number of greased muffin cups half full. Bake in a preheated 400-degree oven for 20 minutes or until light brown. Remove to a wire rack to cool.

You may store the batter in the refrigerator for up to 4 weeks if the batter does not contain applesauce or banana.

Make ahead

CINNAMON BRUNCH BREAD

SERVES 12 TO 16

2 (8-count) cans refrigerator crescent rolls
16 ounces cream cheese, softened
1 cup sugar
1 egg yolk

1 teaspoon vanilla extract
1 egg white, lightly beaten
^{1}/$_2$ cup sugar
1 teaspoon cinnamon
^{1}/$_2$ cup chopped nuts

Unroll one can of crescent dough and fit in the bottom of a greased 9×13-inch baking pan. Press the seams to seal. Beat the cream cheese, 1 cup sugar, egg yolk and vanilla in a mixing bowl. Spread over the dough in the pan. Unroll the remaining can of crescent dough and press the seams to seal. Place on top of the cream cheese mixture. Brush the egg white over the dough. Combine ^{1}/$_2$ cup sugar and the cinnamon in a bowl. Sprinkle over the dough and sprinkle the nuts over the cinnamon mixture. Bake in a preheated 350-degree oven for 30 minutes or until golden brown and puffed. Remove to a wire rack to cool for at least 3 hours before cutting.

Make ahead

GRAND MARNIER FRENCH TOAST

SERVES 8 TO 10

1/2 cup (1 stick) unsalted butter
1 cup packed brown sugar
2 tablespoons corn syrup
6 (1-inch) slices French bread
5 eggs
1 1/2 cups half-and-half
1 teaspoon vanilla extract
2 teaspoons Grand Marnier
1/4 teaspoon salt
Confectioners' sugar
1/2 cup chopped pecans

Melt the butter in a heavy saucepan over medium heat. Add the brown sugar and corn syrup and stir well. Pour evenly over the bottom of an ungreased 9×13-inch baking dish. Arrange the bread slices in a single layer over the brown sugar mixture. Whisk the eggs, half-and-half, vanilla, Grand Marnier and salt in a bowl. Pour evenly over the bread in the baking dish. Chill, covered, for 8 hours to overnight. Let warm, uncovered, to room temperature. Bake in a preheated 350-degree oven for 30 to 40 minutes or until golden brown. Dust with confectioners' sugar and sprinkle with the pecans. Serve with maple syrup on the side.

Make ahead

Pain Perdu

French toast or "lost bread"; so called because it uses day-old French bread that has become dry

OLD-FASHIONED PANCAKES

SERVES 4 TO 6

CINNAMON CREAM SYRUP
1 cup sugar
1/2 cup light corn syrup
1/4 cup water
3/4 to 1 teaspoon cinnamon
1/4 cup evaporated milk

PANCAKES
1 cup all-purpose flour
3/4 to 1 cup milk
1 egg
1 tablespoon sugar
1 teaspoon salt
1 teaspoon baking powder
1 tablespoon shortening

SYRUP
Combine the sugar, corn syrup, water and cinnamon in a saucepan. Bring to
a boil over medium heat, stirring constantly. Boil for 2 to 2 1/2 minutes,
stirring constantly. Remove from the heat and let cool for 5 minutes. Stir in
the evaporated milk. Serve over the pancakes.

PANCAKES
Beat the flour, milk, egg, sugar, salt and baking powder in a mixing bowl.
Melt the shortening on a griddle or in a large nonstick skillet. Add the melted
shortening to the batter and beat well. Pour 1/4 cup at a time onto the hot
griddle. Cook until brown on both sides.

*Bottles with "sticky" contents
(corn syrup, molasses, maple
syrup, jelly etc.) can be a hassle
to keep reopening. So before using
the bottle for the first time, wipe
the threads with a light coating
of oil. The lid will never stick
and won't be difficult to open.*

*When baking, grate butter
on the large-hole side of a cheese
grater instead of cutting it
in with a knife. This makes the
whole process easier and less
messy. Hold the butter by the
wrapper to prevent it from melting
from warmth of your hands.*

CULTURAL CROSSROADS
Entrées

Lake Charles is a community built around a cultural crossroad. Here Cajuns,

Creoles, and cowboys come together to create a lifestyle like no other.

We revel in our Cajun heritage, as it produces a life filled with spice and

exhilaration. Creole roots bestow the gifts of rhythm and joy, as they distinctly

flavor our world. And finally, Southwest Louisiana's cowboys season our

culture with a western flair that makes for great stories and terrific barbecues.

Through the pages of this chapter, we'll introduce popular entrées

influenced by cultural crossroads. You'll find elegant and

old-fashioned dishes, all delectable and all specially chosen to bring

a bit of South Louisiana to your table.

Entrées

Beef Tenderloin en Croûte 71 • Filet of Beef with Green Peppercorns 72

Special Occasion Standing Rib Roast 72 • Saucy Beef Brisket 73 • Balsamic Beef Tenderloin 74

Royal Beef Tenderloin 74 • Individual Beef Wellingtons 75 • Pot Roast with Dumplings 76

Cajun Pot Roast 77 • Asian Flank Steak 77 • Brandied Steak au Poivre 78

Short Ribs Braised in Wine 78 • Jazzy Jambalaya 79 • Stuffed Red Bell Peppers 80

Savory Italian Meat Sauce 80 • Linguini with Meat Sauce 81 • Veal Marsala 81

Roast Rack of Lamb 82 • Grilled Baby Lamb Chops 82 • Herbed Leg of Lamb 83 • Creole Glazed Ham 84

Perfect Pork Roast 85 • Maple- and Pecan-Glazed Pork Tenderloin 85

Molasses Pork Tenderloin 88 • Country Pork and Apples 88

Smothered Pork Chops in Tomato Gravy 89 • Black-Eyed Pea and Sausage Jambalaya 90

Cheddar Cheese Strata 91 • Braised Balsamic Chicken 91 • Chicken in Port 92 • Coq Au Vin 92

India Butter Chicken 93 • Country Fried Chicken 94 • Almond Dijon Chicken 94

Chicken Florentine 95 • Provençal Chicken with Polenta 96 • Arroz Con Pollo 97

Chicken Enchiladas with Green Sauce 98 • Quick Gourmet Chicken Pizza with Arugula 99

Chicken and Avocado Pasta 99 • Cornish Hens "To Die For" 100 • Spinach Phyllo Pie 101

Asparagus Linguini 102 • Fresh Tomato Vermicelli 102 • Vodka and Cream Pasta 103

BEEF TENDERLOIN EN CROÛTE
SERVES 4

1 tablespoon vegetable oil
4 (6-ounce, 1-inch-thick) beef tenderloin filets
1/4 cup pesto
1 sheet frozen puff pastry, thawed
Long green onion strips (optional)

Heat the oil in a skillet over medium-high heat. Add the filets and cook for
1 minute per side or until brown. Remove the filets to paper towels to
drain and let cool slightly. Spread 1 tablespoon pesto over the top of each
filet. Roll out the pastry on a floured work surface to a 12-inch square.
Cut the pastry into four 6-inch squares. Place one pastry square over each
filet and gently tuck the edges of the pastry under the filet. Arrange the
filets, pastry side up, on a rack in a roasting pan lined with foil. Bake in a
preheated 450-degree oven for 12 to 15 minutes or until the pastry is golden
brown and the beef is medium-rare. Wrap green onion strips around each
filet and tie to resemble a package. Serve immediately.

En Croûte
Baked within a crust: traditionally meat or fowl

FILET OF BEEF WITH GREEN PEPPERCORNS
SERVES 6

A simple way to keep stock readily available is to prepare the stock ahead of time and freeze in ice cube trays. After they are frozen, remove and store in a heavy duty plastic bag.

1 (4-pound) filet of beef, trimmed and tied	3 tablespoons drained green peppercorns in brine
2 tablespoons vegetable oil	Lemon juice to taste
Salt and pepper to taste	3 tablespoons butter, softened and cut into small pieces
3 tablespoons Cognac, heated	
1 1/2 cups beef stock	Watercress and decoratively
1 cup heavy cream	cut tomatoes for garnish

Let the beef stand at room temperature for 1 hour. Heat the oil in a heavy skillet over medium-high heat. Add the beef and brown on all sides and season with salt and pepper. Remove the beef to a rack in a shallow roasting pan. Roast in a preheated 450-degree oven for 30 to 35 minutes for medium-rare. Remove the beef to a cutting board and cover loosely with foil. Let stand for 10 minutes. Drain the skillet and add the Cognac. Ignite the Cognac with a long match and carefully shake the pan until the flames die out. Deglaze the skillet by scraping any brown bits from the bottom and sides of the pan. Stir in the stock and cream. Cook over medium-high heat until the mixture is reduced to 2 cups, stirring frequently. Stir in the peppercorns and season with lemon juice, salt and pepper. Remove from the heat and add the butter, swirling the pan until the butter melts. Cut the beef into 1/2-inch slices and arrange on a heated serving platter. Spoon some of the sauce over the beef and garnish with watercress and tomatoes. Serve the remaining sauce on the side.

SPECIAL OCCASION STANDING RIB ROAST
SERVES 25 TO 30

Filet is the French spelling of fillet as it applies to boneless meat, chicken, or fish.

1 (15- to 16-pound) standing rib roast,
cut from the small end
3 to 4 teaspoons salt
Pepper to taste
Beef broth or water

Place the roast, fat side up, in a roasting pan and let come to room temperature. Pat the roast with paper towels to dry. Sprinkle with the salt and season with pepper. Roast in a preheated 325-degree oven for 2 to 2 1/2 hours or to 120 degrees on a meat thermometer for medium-rare. Remove the roast to a cutting board and cover loosely with foil and let stand for 15 to 30 minutes. Skim the fat from the roasting pan. Stir in beef broth to make au jus. Carve the roast and serve the au jus on the side.

SAUCY BEEF BRISKET
SERVES 12

DRY RUB
1 tablespoon chili powder
1 tablespoon seasoned salt
2 teaspoons hickory smoked salt
2 teaspoons cracked pepper
2 teaspoons ground rosemary

BEEF BRISKET
4 cups vegetable oil
1 1/4 cups Worcestershire sauce
1 tablespoon rosemary
1 tablespoon hickory smoked salt
1 tablespoon seasoned salt
1 tablespoon mixed peppercorns
1 (6-pound) boneless beef
   brisket, trimmed

3 or 4 bay leaves
2 cups hickory chips, soaked in
   water for 1 hour

SMOKY SAUCE
1 (14-ounce) bottle ketchup
1 cup plus 1 tablespoon red
   wine vinegar
1 tablespoon brown sugar
1/4 cup Worcestershire sauce
1 teaspoon dried tarragon
2 teaspoons hickory smoked salt
2 teaspoons liquid smoke
Tabasco sauce to taste

DRY RUB
Combine the chili powder, seasoned salt, hickory smoked salt, pepper and rosemary in a jar with a tight-fitting lid and shake well.

BRISKET
Combine the oil, Worcestershire sauce, rosemary, hickory smoked salt, seasoned salt and peppercorns in a blender container. Process at medium speed for 1 minute. Place the brisket in a large pan and add the bay leaves. Pour the oil mixture over the beef. Chill, covered, overnight, turning occasionally. Drain and discard the marinade. Remove the brisket to a work surface. Coat all the sides of the brisket with the dry rub. Place the beef in a shallow dish and chill, covered, overnight.

Build a charcoal fire in a wood smoker. Pierce a 12-inch square sheet of foil several times with a wooden pick. Drain the wood chips and place on the foil. Fold the edges of the foil to make sides. Place the foil packet on the hot coals. Add water to the smoker pan. Place the brisket on the smoker rack. Cook, covered, for 10 to 12 hours without removing the lid of the smoker. Cut the brisket into thin slices and serve with the sauce on the side.

SAUCE
Empty the ketchup into a saucepan. Pour the vinegar into the empty ketchup bottle and shake well. Add the vinegar to the saucepan. Add the brown sugar, Worcestershire sauce, tarragon, hickory smoked salt and liquid smoke. Bring to a simmer over low heat, stirring occasionally. Season with Tabasco sauce.

Make ahead

BALSAMIC BEEF TENDERLOIN

SERVES 8 TO 10

Balsamic vinegar is Italian aromatic vinegar that ages to a full-bodied, dark brown, slightly sweet, slightly tart syrup. It is produced much like a fine wine that is difficult to create and time is a critical ingredient. It can range in price from a few dollars to a few hundred dollars per bottle. This vinegar should be stored away from direct heat and light. It typically has a shelf life of two to three years and does not require refrigeration.

1 (4- to 5-pound) beef tenderloin, trimmed
Olive oil
Cracked black pepper
Garlic powder
Salt
Herbes de Provence
Cayenne pepper
Worcestershire sauce
Balsamic vinegar

Place the beef in a shallow dish and coat with olive oil. Season generously with black pepper and garlic powder. Sprinkle with salt and herbes de Provence. Season lightly with cayenne pepper. Drizzle generously with Worcestershire sauce and sprinkle lightly with balsamic vinegar. Chill, covered, for 24 hours. Remove the beef from the marinade and discard the marinade. Grill over medium-hot coals for 15 minutes, turning the beef every 5 minutes. Remove to a rack in a roasting pan and roast in a preheated 425-degree oven for 15 to 20 minutes for medium-rare. Let the beef stand for 10 minutes before slicing.

You may add wood chips to the coals for a light smoke flavor.

ROYAL BEEF TENDERLOIN

SERVES 16

1 (8-pound) beef tenderloin
Cracked pepper to taste (optional)
2 tablespoons Worcestershire sauce
1/4 cup soy sauce
2 tablespoons Kitchen Bouquet

Place the beef in a shallow dish and coat with pepper. Mix the Worcestershire sauce, soy sauce and Kitchen Bouquet in a bowl. Pour over the tenderloin, turning the beef to coat all sides. Chill, covered, for 2 to 3 hours, turning the beef occasionally. Remove the beef to a rack in a foil-lined roasting pan and discard the marinade. Roast in a preheated 400-degree oven for 15 minutes. Turn off the heat but do not open the oven door for 20 minutes for a medium-rare roast.

INDIVIDUAL BEEF WELLINGTONS
SERVES 8

8 (6-ounce, 1 1/2-inch-thick) center-cut filets mignons
Salt and freshly ground pepper to taste
2 tablespoons olive oil
2 tablespoons minced shallots
2 tablespoons unsalted butter
4 large button mushrooms, thinly sliced
4 large portabellini mushrooms, thinly sliced
2 tablespoons minced garlic
1/8 teaspoon dried thyme
1/8 teaspoon dried oregano
2 sheets frozen puff pastry, thawed
1/2 cup crumbled Gorgonzola cheese
2 eggs, lightly beaten
2 cups veal demi-glace or beef demi-glace
1/4 cup madeira or red wine

Pat the filets mignons dry with a paper towel and season with salt and pepper. Heat the olive oil in a skillet. Add the beef and brown on both sides. Remove to a platter. Chill, covered, for 1 hour or until cold. Sauté the shallots in the butter in a heavy skillet for 1 minute. Add the button mushrooms, portabellini mushrooms, garlic, thyme and oregano and season with salt and pepper. Sauté until the mushrooms are light brown. Remove the mixture to a bowl and let cool completely.

Roll out each pastry sheet on a lightly floured work surface to a 14-inch square. Trim 1-inch from the edges to make two 13-inch squares. Cut each into four 6 1/2-inch squares. Place 1 tablespoon cheese on the center of each pastry square and top with one-eighth of the mushroom mixture. Top each with one filet, pressing gently. Pull two opposite corners of each pastry square over the beef, overlapping the edges. Brush with beaten egg. Repeat with the two remaining corners. Brush any gaps with beaten egg to seal. Arrange seam side down in a nonstick roasting pan.

Chill, loosely covered, for 1 to 24 hours. Brush with the remaining beaten egg. Bake in a preheated 425-degree oven for 20 to 30 minutes or until the pastry is golden brown and the beef registers 117 degrees on a meat thermometer. Combine the demi-glace and madeira in a saucepan. Bring to a boil and boil for 1 minute. Serve warm on the side.

Make ahead

PORCHES AND VERANDAS
Porch culture is alive and well in Southwest Louisiana because many homes still feature porches and verandas, our architectural staples. Historically, before air conditioning was standard in homes, these areas provided an opportunity for a cool, shaded spot on a hot summer day. Today, as in years past, porches provide a place for gathering in celebration, conversation, or simply in contemplation.

POT ROAST WITH DUMPLINGS
SERVES 8

POT ROAST
1 (3- to 4-pound) beef pot roast
Salt to taste
All-purpose flour
2 garlic cloves, crushed
1/4 cup (1/2 stick) butter
1 large onion, thinly sliced
12 peppercorns
12 whole cloves
1 bay leaf, crumbled
1 tablespoon grated horseradish
1/2 cup good-quality rum or dry red wine
1/2 cup water
Baby carrots (optional)

DUMPLINGS
2 cups all-purpose flour
4 teaspoons baking powder
1/2 teaspoon salt
1 scant cup milk

ROAST
Rub the beef with salt and flour. Sauté the garlic in the butter in a skillet.
Add the beef and brown on all sides. Arrange the onion over the bottom of
a Dutch oven. Place the beef over the onions and add the sautéed garlic and
butter. Add the peppercorns, cloves, bay leaf and horseradish. Pour the rum
over the top. Simmer, covered, for 3 to 4 hours or until the meat is tender.
Add the water gradually during cooking and add carrots 30 minutes before
the meat is done.

DUMPLINGS
Sift the flour, baking powder and salt into a bowl. Add the milk and mix well.
Drop by spoonfuls into the pot roast liquid and simmer for last 12 minutes.

Cajun Pot Roast

Serves 6

1 (3-pound) beef sirloin or chuck roast
2 large garlic cloves, cut into 1/4 to 1/2-inch pieces
3 cayenne chiles or jalapeño chiles, cut into 1/4 to 1/2-inch pieces
Salt and pepper to taste
1 large onion, chopped
1 bell pepper, chopped
1 large garlic clove, minced
1 (4-ounce) can whole or sliced mushrooms
1 tablespoon Worcestershire sauce
Creole seasoning to taste

Cut 1/2 to 3/4-inch slits into the beef. Stuff one piece of garlic and one piece of chile into each slit. Season the roast with salt and pepper. Heat a large heavy nonstick saucepan over medium heat. Add the beef and brown well on all sides. Add the onion, bell pepper and minced garlic and sauté until tender. Add water to the saucepan to cover the beef. Stir in the mushrooms and Worcestershire sauce and season with Creole seasoning. Simmer, covered, for 3 to 4 hours or until tender, adding additional water if needed to keep the liquid level halfway up the beef.

You may stir 1 tablespoon all-purpose flour mixed with 1 cup cold water into the liquid near the end of cooking for a thicker gravy.

To seed a jalapeno without wearing gloves, cut off both ends of the chile. Stand it on a cutting board and slice down its sides, removing the flesh around the core. Discard the core with the seeds.

Asian Flank Steak

Serves 4

1 pound lean flank steak, trimmed
1/4 cup sherry
1/4 cup low-sodium soy sauce
1/4 cup honey
2 tablespoons white vinegar
1 tablespoon minced fresh ginger
1 teaspoon dark sesame oil
2 garlic cloves, crushed

Combine the steak, sherry, soy sauce, honey, vinegar, ginger, sesame oil and garlic in a sealable plastic bag. Seal the bag and turn to mix. Chill for 8 hours to overnight, turning occasionally. Remove the steak and reserve the marinade. Place the steak on a grill or broiler rack coated with nonstick cooking spray. Broil or grill for 8 minutes per side or to the desired doneness, basting frequently with the marinade. Pour the remaining marinade into a saucepan and bring to a boil. Cook over medium heat for 1 minute. Slice the steak diagonally and serve with the warm marinade.

BRANDIED STEAK AU POIVRE

SERVES 4

1 teaspoon cracked pepper	¹/₈ teaspoon onion powder
³/₄ teaspoon chopped fresh basil, or	4 beef cubed steaks
¹/₄ teaspoon dried basil	1 tablespoon butter or margarine
³/₄ teaspoon chopped fresh rosemary,	2 tablespoons brandy or beef broth
or ¹/₄ teaspoon dried rosemary	¹/₄ cup beef broth

Mix the pepper, basil, rosemary and onion powder in a bowl. Rub into all sides of the steaks. Melt the butter in a skillet. Add the steaks and cook for 7 to 8 minutes for medium-rare, turning occasionally. Remove the steaks to a platter and keep warm. Add the brandy and broth to the skillet and heat to boiling, scraping any brown bits from the bottom of the pan. Reduce the heat to low and simmer for 3 to 4 minutes or until slightly thickened. Pour over the steaks and serve.

SHORT RIBS BRAISED IN WINE

SERVES 6

4 pounds beef short ribs, trimmed	2 cups red wine
1 teaspoon salt	1 bay leaf
1 teaspoon pepper	1 sprig fresh thyme
1 tablespoon vegetable oil	1 (14-ounce) can beef broth
1 onion, chopped	4 large carrots, cut into 2-inch pieces
5 garlic cloves, minced	2 turnips, cut into 2-inch pieces
2 tablespoons tomato paste	Hot cooked egg noodles or rice

Sprinkle the ribs with the salt and pepper. Heat the oil in a large Dutch oven over medium-high heat until hot. Add half the ribs and cook for 10 minutes or until brown, turning once or twice. Remove the ribs to a platter. Add the remaining ribs and repeat. Add the onion and garlic to the pan and sauté for 3 minutes. Stir in the tomato paste and cook for 2 minutes. Stir in the wine, bay leaf and thyme and bring to a boil. Add the ribs and broth and reduce the heat. Simmer, covered, for 2 hours. Add the carrots and turnips and bring to a boil. Reduce the heat and simmer, covered, for 1 hour and 15 minutes or until the meat and vegetables are very tender. Remove the bay leaf and thyme sprig and serve over hot egg noodles or rice.

JAZZY JAMBALAYA
SERVES 6

1 pound ground beef or turkey
2 tablespoons olive oil
1/2 cup chopped onion
1/2 cup chopped bell pepper
1 cup rice
1 (15-ounce) can black beans
1 (10-ounce) can tomatoes with green chiles
1 1/2 cups frozen corn kernels
1 (15-ounce) can chicken stock or beef stock
Creole seasoning to taste
Salt to taste
Chopped fresh cilantro

Brown the ground beef in a skillet, stirring until crumbly; drain. Wipe the skillet with a paper towel to remove any grease. Add the olive oil, onion and bell pepper to the skillet and sauté for 3 minutes. Add the rice and cook for 2 minutes, stirring frequently. Stir in the black beans, tomatoes with green chiles, corn and stock. Season with Creole seasoning and salt and reduce the heat to low. Cook, covered, for 20 minutes. Sprinkle with cilantro and serve with corn bread and a green salad.

Jambalaya

A mixture of rice, Louisiana seasonings, and beef, pork, or chicken. This traditional dish is a Louisiana version of the famous Spanish paella.

STUFFED RED BELL PEPPERS
SERVES 4

4 red bell peppers
1/4 cup extra-virgin olive oil
1 yellow or Vidalia onion, chopped
6 garlic cloves, chopped
1 pound ground chuck
1 1/2 cups cooked rice

1 cup canned tomatoes with
   green chiles
1 tablespoon chopped fresh oregano
Salt and freshly ground pepper
   to taste
1/2 cup ketchup

Cut 1-inch from the stem end of the bell peppers and remove the seeds. Add the bell peppers to a large saucepan of boiling salted water. Boil the bell peppers until tender-crisp, pushing with a spoon to keep the bell peppers submerged in the boiling water. Drain the peppers and let cool. Heat the olive oil in a large skillet over medium heat. Add the onion and garlic and sauté until tender and golden brown. Add the ground beef and brown, stirring until crumbly. Drain and remove from the heat. Add the rice, tomatoes with green chiles and oregano. Season with salt and pepper and mix well. Spoon the filling into the bell peppers. Arrange the stuffed bell peppers, cut side up, in a baking dish. Mix the ketchup with 6 tablespoons water in a bowl and spoon over the peppers. Add 3 to 4 tablespoons water to the baking dish. Bake in a preheated 350-degree oven for 1 hour, basting once or twice with the cooking liquid.

SAVORY ITALIAN MEAT SAUCE
SERVES 6

2 tablespoons olive oil
2 cups finely chopped onions
1/2 cup finely chopped bell pepper
1/2 cup finely chopped celery
1 pound ground round or
   ground chuck
4 to 8 ounces hot Italian sausage,
   casings removed
4 garlic cloves, pressed
1 teaspoon salt
2 teaspoons chili powder

1/2 teaspoon ground oregano
1/2 teaspoon dried basil
   leaves, crushed
1/4 teaspoon white pepper
1 1/2 cups beef stock
1 (6-ounce) can tomato paste
1 (8-ounce) can tomatoes with
   green chiles
Freshly grated nutmeg
   to taste
Hot cooked pasta

Heat the olive oil in a heavy 4-quart saucepan. Add the onions, bell pepper and celery and sauté for 5 minutes. Add the ground beef, sausage, garlic, salt, chili powder, oregano, basil and white pepper. Cook for 15 minutes, stirring frequently. Stir in the stock, tomato paste and tomatoes with green chiles. Season with nutmeg. Simmer, covered, for 15 minutes, stirring frequently. Serve over hot cooked pasta.

Make ahead

Linguini with Meat Sauce

Serves 8

2 pounds lean ground beef
2 garlic cloves, minced
1 (28-ounce) can crushed tomatoes
1 (8-ounce) can tomato sauce
1 (6-ounce) can tomato paste
1 teaspoon salt
2 teaspoons sugar

2 cups sour cream
8 ounces cream cheese, softened
8 ounces linguini, cooked
    al dente and drained
2 cups (8 ounces) shredded
    sharp Cheddar cheese

When cooking pasta . . . add salt to water . . . but not oil! The sauce will stick better if you don't use oil.

Brown the ground beef with the garlic in a heavy saucepan, stirring until crumbly; drain. Stir in the tomatoes, tomato sauce, tomato paste, salt and sugar. Simmer for 30 minutes and remove from the heat. Combine the sour cream and cream cheese in a large bowl and mix well. Add the cooked pasta and mix well. Spread the pasta mixture over the bottom of a lightly greased 9×13-inch baking dish. Top evenly with the meat sauce. Bake in a preheated 350-degree oven for 20 to 25 minutes or until heated through. Sprinkle with the Cheddar cheese and bake for 5 minutes longer or until the cheese is melted. Let stand for 5 minutes before serving.

   This recipe may be made ahead without the Cheddar cheese and frozen. Thaw overnight in the refrigerator and let stand at room temperature for 30 minutes before adding the Cheddar cheese and baking.

 Make ahead

Veal Marsala

Serves 4

1 pound veal scallopini,
thinly sliced and pounded flat
3/4 cup all-purpose flour
3 tablespoons (or more)
    vegetable oil

Salt and freshly ground pepper
    to taste
3/4 cup dry marsala
3 tablespoons butter

To get rid of baked-on food, fill the container with water and place a Bounce laundry softener sheet in the bowl and soak overnight. The static from the Bounce sheet will cause the baked on food to adhere to it. You may perform the same procedure with two Efferdent tablets.

Dredge the veal in the flour and shake off any excess. Heat the oil in a heavy skillet over medium-high heat. Brown the veal in the skillet a few pieces at a time, adding more oil, if needed. Remove the veal to a platter and season with salt and pepper. Turn the heat to high and add the marsala to the skillet. Boil for 1 minute, scraping any brown bits from the bottom of the pan. Add the butter and any juices from the cooked veal that have collected on the platter. Cook until the sauce thickens, stirring constantly. Add the veal and cook until heated through. Serve immediately.

ROAST RACK OF LAMB

SERVES 2

1 (8-rib) rack of lamb, trimmed	1/2 teaspoon chopped
Salt and pepper to taste	fresh rosemary
1/2 cup Dijon mustard	1/2 teaspoon chopped fresh chives
1/2 cup finely crushed	1/2 teaspoon chopped fresh parsley
saltine crackers	

Bring the lamb to room temperature and season with salt and pepper. Spread the Dijon mustard evenly over the top and sides of the lamb. Combine the cracker crumbs, rosemary, chives and parsley in a bowl and mix well. Sprinkle over the mustard coating. Place the lamb, bone side down, on a rack in a roasting pan. Roast in the center of a preheated 400-degree oven for 30 to 35 minutes for medium. Add a small amount of water to the roasting pan if excess crumbs begin to burn. Remove the lamb to a cutting board and let stand for 10 minutes before slicing.

GRILLED BABY LAMB CHOPS

SERVES 2

1 teaspoon dry mustard	5 tablespoons good-quality
1/2 teaspoon salt	olive oil
1/4 teaspoon paprika	1 rack of lamb, trimmed and
4 garlic cloves, pressed	cut into chops
3 tablespoons balsamic vinegar	

Combine the dry mustard, salt, paprika, garlic, vinegar and olive oil in a shallow dish and mix well. Add the lamb chops and turn to coat. Chill, covered, for 3 hours to overnight, turning once. Remove the lamb chops and reserve the marinade. Grill the lamb chops over a hot fire for 5 minutes per side for medium-rare, basting occasionally with the marinade. Discard any remaining marinade.

 Make ahead

HERBED LEG OF LAMB
SERVES 6

1 (7-pound) leg of lamb
2 peeled garlic bulbs, cut into slivers (peelings reserved)
1 tablespoon oregano
1 tablespoon thyme
$1/4$ teaspoon rosemary
2 teaspoons sea salt
2 teaspoons freshly ground pepper
5 garlic cloves, minced (peelings reserved)
$1/4$ cup extra-virgin olive oil
6 unpeeled garlic bulbs, stem end removed
Onion peelings (reserved from another recipe)
Carrot peelings (reserved from another recipe)
2 bay leaves
1 cup chardonnay
1 tablespoon fresh thyme
1 cup red wine

Cut $1/2$-inch slits into the lamb near the center of the leg and insert the garlic slivers into the slits. Combine the oregano, 1 tablespoon thyme, the rosemary, salt, pepper, minced garlic and olive oil in a bowl and mix well. Rub the herb mixture into all sides and creases of the lamb. Place the lamb, rounded side up, in a 13×18-inch roasting pan. Roast on the second rack from the bottom in a preheated 500-degree oven for 15 minutes. Add the unpeeled garlic bulbs, reserved garlic peelings, onion peelings, carrot peelings, bay leaves, chardonnay and 1 tablespoon fresh thyme to the roasting pan. Roast for 30 minutes longer or to medium-rare.

Remove the lamb to a platter and keep warm. Strain the pan juices into a container and discard the solids. Skim the fat from the strained juices. Add the red wine to the roasting pan and deglaze the pan over medium heat. Stir in the strained pan juices and cook until heated through. Serve with the lamb.

CREOLE GLAZED HAM

1 cup Creole mustard
1 cup packed brown sugar
1 (12-ounce) can root beer
1/2 cup Louisiana cane syrup
1/4 cup pineapple juice
1/4 cup cracked pepper
Pinch of cinnamon
Pinch of nutmeg
Pinch of allspice
Pinch of cloves
1 (5-pound) cured ham

Combine the Creole mustard, brown sugar, root beer, cane syrup and pineapple juice in a bowl and mix well. Whisk in the pepper, cinnamon, nutmeg, allspice and cloves. Place the ham in a 9×13-inch baking pan coated with nonstick cooking spray. Coat the ham with the mustard mixture. Bake in a preheated 350-degree oven for 1 hour, basting twice with the glaze. Bake for 30 minutes longer or until the glaze is thickened and sticky.

Creole mustard

A mustard, which typifies the German influence in Louisiana with vinegar-marinated brown mustard seeds

PERFECT PORK ROAST

SERVES 8 TO 10

1 (12-rib) pork roast, cut from the
small end (about 9 pounds)
Salt and pepper to taste
1 cup good-quality dry red wine
1 cup water
1 cup thinly sliced onion
1 garlic clove, pressed

Bring the pork to room temperature. Pat dry with paper towels and season with salt and pepper. Place the roast in a deep roasting pan, fat side up. Brown the roast in a preheated 400-degree oven or under a broiler. Add the red wine, water, onion and garlic to the roasting pan and cover tightly. Roast in a preheated 325-degree oven for 2 hours or to 165 degrees on a meat thermometer, basting frequently. Brown the roast, uncovered, under a broiler, if desired. Remove the roast to a cutting board and cover loosely with foil. Cook the pan drippings until reduced, scraping any brown bits from the bottom of the pan. Skim the fat from the pan drippings and serve with the roast.

Ask your butcher to crack the bones but not cut through the meat to make carving easier.

MAPLE- AND PECAN-GLAZED PORK TENDERLOIN

SERVES 6

1/2 cup chopped pecans
1/2 cup real maple syrup
2 tablespoons
stone-ground mustard
2 tablespoons bourbon
2 (1-pound) pork tenderloins
1/2 teaspoon salt
1 tablespoon butter
or margarine
1 tablespoon vegetable oil

Syrup or honey can be tough to remove from measuring cups and spoons. One technique is to oil the utensil before measuring—the sticky ingredient will slide out cleanly. Another trick is to use heat. Simply dip the measuring spoon in hot water. Honey will not stick to a heated spoon.

Bring the pecans, maple syrup and stone-ground mustard to a boil in a saucepan, stirring frequently. Reduce the heat and simmer for 3 minutes or until thickened. Stir in the bourbon and remove from the heat.

Sprinkle the pork tenderloins with the salt. Heat the butter and oil in a large ovenproof skillet over medium-high heat. Add the tenderloins and cook for 3 minutes per side or until brown. Spread the maple sauce over the tenderloins and place the skillet in a preheated 450-degree oven. Bake for 12 to 15 minutes or to 160 degrees on a meat thermometer. Remove the tenderloins to a serving platter and cover loosely with foil. Let stand for 10 minutes. Slice the pork and serve with the sauce remaining in the skillet.

MOLASSES PORK TENDERLOIN

SERVES 4 TO 6

1/4 cup molasses
2 tablespoons stone-ground Dijon or Creole mustard
1 tablespoon cider vinegar
2 (12- to 16-ounce) pork tenderloins, trimmed

Combine the molasses, Dijon mustard and vinegar in a bowl and mix well. Brush over the tenderloins on a plate. Chill, covered, for 8 hours. Grill the tenderloins, covered, over medium-hot coals for 10 minutes per side or to 160 degrees on a meat thermometer inserted in the thickest portion of the tenderloins.

Make ahead

COUNTRY PORK AND APPLES

SERVES 6

1/2 cup apple jelly
1/2 cup barbecue sauce
1/4 cup (1/2 stick) butter
2 pounds pork butt or country-style ribs, trimmed
3 Granny Smith apples, cored and cut into wedges
1 teaspoon lemon juice
Salt and pepper to taste

Combine the jelly, barbecue sauce and butter in a saucepan. Cook over low heat until heated through, stirring constantly; keep warm.

Cut the pork into 1-inch cubes or single ribs. Combine the apple wedges and lemon juice in a bowl and toss to coat. Arrange the pork and apples in a single layer in a 9×13-inch baking pan. Season with salt and pepper. Bake in a preheated 350-degree oven for 15 to 20 minutes. Turn the pork and apples over and broil for 10 minutes. Turn over and repeat. Brush with half of the sauce. Broil on each side for 10 minutes. Remove from the oven. Brush with the remaining sauce and serve.

SMOTHERED PORK CHOPS IN TOMATO GRAVY

SERVES 6

8 thick center-cut pork chops
Calcasieu seasoning mix to taste (page 163)
1 tablespoon Prudhomme's Meat Magic seasoning
3 slices bacon
3 tablespoons tomato paste
2 onions, chopped
6 garlic cloves, minced
1 cup chopped celery
6 carrots, cut into 1/2-inch slices
1 red bell pepper, sliced into rings
1 yellow bell pepper, sliced into rings
1/4 cup minced flat-leaf parsley
1 (16-ounce) can no-salt-added diced tomatoes
12 fresh button mushrooms, sliced
1 teaspoon whole cloves
2 tablespoons Calcasieu seasoning mix (page 163)
3/4 cup shiraz
1/4 cup shiraz
Hot cooked noodles

Season the pork chops with seasoning mix and the Meat Magic seasoning. Cook the bacon in a 10-inch cast-iron saucepan until crisp. Remove the bacon with a slotted spoon to paper towels to drain; crumble. Add the pork chops to the bacon drippings and brown on both sides. Remove the pork chops to a plate and add the tomato paste to the saucepan. Simmer until the tomato paste is brown, stirring frequently. Add the onions, garlic, celery, carrots, red bell pepper, yellow bell pepper and parsley. Sauté over medium heat until tender. Stir in the tomatoes, mushrooms, cloves, crumbled bacon and 2 tablespoons seasoning mix. Simmer for 1 hour. Stir in 3/4 cup wine and add the pork chops. Bake in a preheated 300-degree oven for 1 hour or to 170 degrees on a meat thermometer inserted in the thickest portion of the pork chops. Stir in 1/4 cup wine and serve over noodles.

CAJUN AND CREOLE

Cajun (derived from the word Acadian) and Creole are terms used to describe some of the people who live in Southwest Louisiana and the variety of French that many of them speak. Cajuns descended from the French who migrated to Nova Scotia and settled in Louisiana in the 17th century. Creoles, on the other hand, are people of Old World ancestry, both French and Spanish, who were born in the New World. Interestingly, nowadays, "Creole" also refers to a language evolved from pidgin zed French, a sort of colloquial lingo, which is spoken by some South Louisiana black communities who maintain the customs, languages, and traditions of their ancestors.

Although the early Cajun settlers maintained a distinct culture and use of their native language, Native Americans, Spaniards, and Creoles soon influenced them. This melding of people and traditions joyously gives us the music and cuisine we enjoy today.

At one time linguists could distinguish between "colonial" French, Acadian French, and Creole French, but today colonial and Acadian French have become a unique "Cajun" variety. French speaking people from other countries can understand the majority of Cajun words and structures.

BLACK-EYED PEA AND SAUSAGE JAMBALAYA

SERVES 4

1 bag frozen onion, bell pepper and parsley mix
1/2 cup (1 stick) butter
1 1/4 cups rice
1 can black-eyed peas with jalapeño chiles
1 pound sausage links, sliced
1 cup beef broth

Sauté the frozen onion, bell pepper and parsley mix in the butter in a saucepan until tender. Stir in the rice, black-eyed peas with jalapeño chiles, sausage and broth. Simmer, covered, until the rice is tender.

Hoppin' John
Black-eyed peas cooked with pork.
This dish originated with African slaves
on Southern plantations and is now a traditional
New Year's Day dish promising to bring good luck

CHEDDAR CHEESE STRATA
SERVES 8

1 pound bulk pork sausage
8 eggs
3 cups milk
2 tablespoons all-purpose flour
2 tablespoons butter, melted
1 teaspoon salt
¼ teaspoon pepper
Favorite seasonings to taste
1 (8-ounce) package fresh
   mushrooms, sliced

1 (8-ounce) package frozen
   asparagus spears, thawed
   and sliced
2 cups (8 ounces) shredded
   Cheddar cheese
½ cup (2 ounces) grated
   Parmesan cheese
8 cups bread (1-inch cubes)

Brown the sausage in a skillet, stirring until crumbly; drain. Whisk the eggs, milk, flour, butter, salt and pepper in a large bowl. Whisk in your favorite seasonings. Stir in the cooked sausage, mushrooms, asparagus, Cheddar cheese, Parmesan cheese and bread cubes. Spoon into an ungreased 9×13-inch baking dish. Cover with plastic wrap and chill overnight. Place the baking dish on a baking sheet and remove plastic wrap. Bake in the middle of a preheated 350-degree oven for 1 hour.

 Make ahead

BRAISED BALSAMIC CHICKEN
SERVES 6

1 roasting chicken, cut up
Sea salt and freshly ground pepper
   to taste
1 tablespoon olive oil
2 large onions, thinly sliced
5 garlic cloves, sliced
½ cup balsamic vinegar
8 ounces green beans, cut into halves

½ cup canned tomatoes with
   green chiles
1 pound small potatoes, peeled
   and halved
½ cup pitted green olives,
   coarsely chopped
1 teaspoon dried rosemary

Season the chicken with salt and pepper. Heat the olive oil in an 8-inch cast-iron Dutch oven. Add the chicken and brown on all sides. Remove the chicken to a plate and drain the excess fat from the pan. Add the onions and garlic to the pan. Cook, covered, over medium-low heat for 30 to 45 minutes or until the onions are tender and dark brown, stirring every 5 minutes. Stir in the vinegar, green beans, tomatoes with green chiles, potatoes, olives and rosemary and add the chicken. Bake, covered, in a preheated 325-degree oven for 1 hour and 15 minutes or until the chicken is cooked through.

Chicken in Port

Serves 4 to 6

A bouquet garni is a mixture
of herbs that are placed into
savory foods as they cook to
enhance flavor. A bouquet garni
may either be made from fresh
ingredients tied together or dried
ingredients mixed and placed in
cheesecloth tied into a bag for
dipping into soups, stews, sauces,
casseroles, or meat dishes.

2 sprigs fresh thyme
2 sprigs fresh rosemary
1 sprig fresh oregano
4 fresh sweet basil leaves
2 bay leaves
1 roasting chicken, cut up
Prudhommes's Poultry Magic
seasoning to taste
All-purpose flour
1/4 cup (or more) extra-virgin
olive oil

1 yellow onion, coarsely
chopped
2 ounces venison or pork
smoked sausage, finely
chopped
2 garlic cloves, minced
1/2 cup port
2 cups fresh mushrooms
4 1/2 teaspoons Savoie's roux
4 small green onions, minced

Tie the thyme, rosemary, oregano, basil and bay leaves in a piece of cheesecloth
with cotton twine to make a bouquet garni. Season the chicken with Poultry
Magic seasoning and dredge in flour. Heat the olive oil in an 8-inch cast-iron
Dutch oven to 375 degrees. Add the chicken and brown on all sides. Remove
the chicken to a platter. Add about 2 tablespoons olive oil to the pan, if needed.
Add the onion and sausage and sauté until the onion is tender. Add the garlic
and sauté until the garlic is beginning to brown. Stir in the port and add the
chicken. Stir in the mushrooms and bouquet garni. Cook, covered, over medium-
low heat for 20 minutes. Add the roux and cook until dissolved, stirring
constantly. Simmer, covered, for 35 minutes. Add the green onions and cook
for 15 to 20 minutes or until the chicken is tender and cooked through.
Remove the bouquet garni and serve.

Coq Au Vin

Serves 4

1 pound fresh mushrooms,
sliced
4 whole chicken breasts
2 tablespoons cornstarch
1/4 cup water

3/4 cup rosé or red wine
1/4 cup soy sauce
1 garlic clove, crushed
2 tablespoons olive oil
2 teaspoons brown sugar

Spread the mushrooms over the bottom of a baking dish and top with the
chicken. Dissolve the cornstarch in the water in a bowl. Add the wine, soy
sauce, garlic, olive oil and brown sugar and mix well. Pour over the chicken
in the baking dish. Bake in a preheated 350-degree oven for 1 1/2 hours or
until the chicken is cooked through. Serve with wild rice, cooked green beans
and a tossed salad. The sauce is also good served over broiled steak.

INDIA BUTTER CHICKEN
SERVES 8

1 cup plain yogurt
1/4 cup white vinegar
1/4 cup canola oil
1/2 cup heavy cream
4 garlic cloves, pressed
2 tablespoons minced fresh ginger
1 tablespoon cumin
1 tablespoon garam masala
1 tablespoon freshly ground black pepper
1 teaspoon cayenne pepper
2 teaspoons sea salt
8 skinless chicken thighs or breasts
8 Roma tomatoes, finely chopped
1/2 cup (1 stick) unsalted butter
1/2 teaspoon sea salt
1 teaspoon freshly ground black pepper
3/4 cup heavy cream
1/2 jalapeño chile, seeded and julienned
1 tablespoon coriander
14 cardamom pods, ground and
chaff removed

Combine the yogurt, vinegar, canola oil, 1/2 cup cream, the garlic, ginger,
cumin, garam masala, 1 tablespoon black pepper, the cayenne pepper and
2 teaspoons salt in a large bowl and mix well. Add the chicken and mix to
coat all sides. Remove the coated chicken to a sealable plastic bag. Seal the
bag and chill overnight. Remove the chicken to a shallow roasting pan and
discard any remaining marinade. Bake in a preheated 400-degree oven for
25 minutes. Turn the chicken over and bake for 20 minutes longer or until the
chicken is cooked through.

Cook the tomatoes in a wok or large sauté pan until the liquid has evaporated,
stirring frequently. Stir in the butter, 1/2 teaspoon salt, 1 teaspoon black
pepper, 3/4 cup cream, the jalapeño chile, coriander and cardamom and simmer
for 5 minutes. Add the chicken and simmer for 5 minutes, turning the chicken
once. Serve with hot cooked rice.

COUNTRY FRIED CHICKEN
SERVES 4

Tabasco sauce (optional)	3/4 cup evaporated milk
4 split chicken breasts, cut in half or your favorite chicken pieces	1/2 cup water
	1 egg, lightly beaten
Salt and freshly ground pepper to taste	All-purpose flour for dredging
	Peanut oil for frying

Rub a couple of drops of Tabasco sauce under the skin of each chicken breast and season with salt and pepper. Whisk the evaporated milk, water and egg in a shallow bowl and season with salt and pepper. Dip the chicken in the milk mixture and coat in flour. Heat peanut oil to 350 degrees in a cast-iron skillet. Fry the chicken in the hot oil until golden brown on all sides and cooked through.

ALMOND DIJON CHICKEN
SERVES 4

2/3 cup sliced almonds	2 cups heavy whipping cream
1 tablespoon butter	3 tablespoons (or more) orange marmalade
4 boneless skinless chicken breast halves, or 12 to 16 chicken tenders	1/4 teaspoon (or more) cayenne pepper
Salt and black pepper to taste	1 package long grain and wild rice mix, cooked according to package directions
Garlic powder to taste	
1/4 cup (1/2 stick) butter	
2 tablespoons (or more) Dijon mustard	

Sauté the almonds in 1 tablespoon butter in a skillet until light brown. Flatten thick chicken breasts between sheets of waxed paper with a meat mallet. Season the chicken with salt, black pepper and garlic powder. Melt 1/4 cup butter in a skillet over medium-high heat. Add the chicken and brown on both sides. Reduce the heat to medium and stir in the Dijon mustard, cream, marmalade and cayenne pepper. Cook for 10 to 15 minutes or until the sauce is thickened and the chicken is cooked through, stirring frequently. Do not boil. Stir in 1/2 cup of the almonds. Serve over the rice and top with the remaining almonds.

CHICKEN FLORENTINE
SERVES 6

3 (10-ounce) packages frozen spinach
1 (14-ounce) can quartered
artichoke hearts, drained (optional)
6 boneless skinless chicken breasts
$1/2$ cup (1 stick) butter, melted
Creole seasoning to taste
All-purpose flour for dredging
2 tablespoons all-purpose flour
2 cups half-and-half (may use fat free)
$1^1/2$ cups (6 ounces) grated Parmesan
cheese (may use reduced fat)
Paprika

Cook the spinach in a saucepan of boiling salted water according to the package directions. Drain the spinach and squeeze dry. Spread the spinach over the bottom of an 11×13-inch baking dish coated with nonstick cooking spray. Spread the artichokes over the spinach. Coat the chicken breasts in the melted butter and season with Creole seasoning. Dredge the chicken breasts in flour and arrange over the artichokes in the baking dish. Sprinkle 2 tablespoons flour over the chicken. Pour the half-and-half evenly over the chicken. Top with the cheese and sprinkle with paprika. Bake in a preheated 375-degree oven for 45 minutes or until the chicken is cooked through and golden brown.

Poulet
a French "Spring Chicken"

PROVENÇAL CHICKEN WITH POLENTA
SERVES 4 TO 6

Polenta is a boiled, slow-cooked cornmeal "mush"—typically made with coarsely ground yellow corn meal. Cooled and hardened, polenta can be sliced, sautéed, or grilled, and served sweet or savory. It is delicious if homemade but is also available in tubes at many grocery stores.

PROVENÇAL CHICKEN
4 to 6 large boneless skinless chicken breasts,
cut into strips
Salt and pepper to taste
3 tablespoons olive oil
1 onion, chopped
4 garlic cloves, chopped
1/2 cup white wine
1 cup low-sodium chicken stock
1 (10-ounce) can condensed cream of
mushroom soup
1 large can mushrooms, drained
1/2 teaspoon dried thyme
1/2 teaspoon dried rosemary

POLENTA
6 cups low-sodium chicken stock
2 teaspoons salt
1 3/4 cups yellow cornmeal
6 tablespoons butter
3/4 cup (3 ounces) grated Parmesan cheese
1 tablespoon chopped parsley
1/2 teaspoon pepper

CHICKEN
Season the chicken with salt and pepper. Brown the chicken in the olive oil in a large skillet. Remove the chicken to a plate and add the onion to the skillet. Sauté for a few minutes. Add the garlic and sauté for 1 minute. Stir in the wine, stock, soup, mushrooms, thyme and rosemary. Add the chicken and cook over low heat for 15 to 20 minutes or until the chicken is cooked through.

POLENTA
Bring the stock to a boil in a saucepan and add the salt. Whisk in the cornmeal slowly. Bring to a slow boil and cook for 15 minutes, stirring constantly. Remove from the heat and stir in the butter, cheese, parsley and pepper. Spoon the polenta onto serving plates and top with the chicken mixture. Serve with cooked Italian green beans and French bread.

ARROZ CON POLLO

SERVES 8

3 chickens, cut up
1/4 cup Calcasieu seasoning mix (page 163)
1/2 cup extra-virgin olive oil
4 onions, chopped
4 garlic cloves, minced
4 ribs celery, chopped
2 green bell peppers, julienned
1 (28-ounce) can whole tomatoes, drained and chopped
2 bay leaves
4 cups chicken stock
3 cups rice
2 teaspoons salt
1 pinch of saffron threads
1 (6-ounce) jar sliced pimentos
1 cup cooked green peas
1/2 cup chopped flat-leaf parsley

Season the chicken pieces with the seasoning mix and let stand for 30 minutes.
Brown the chicken in the olive oil in a skillet. Remove the chicken to a platter
and add the onions, garlic and celery to the skillet. Sauté until golden brown.
Remove the cooked vegetables to a large Dutch oven. Add the chicken,
bell peppers, tomatoes, bay leaves and stock. Bring to a boil and stir in the rice,
salt and saffron. Reduce the heat and cover. Simmer for 15 minutes, stirring
frequently. Place the covered pan in a preheated 350-degree oven and bake for
45 minutes. Stir in the pimentos, peas and parsley. Cook, covered, for 5 minutes.
Remove the bay leaves and serve immediately.

Audubon
Golf Trails
A collection of golf courses throughout
Louisiana named for the artist, John James Audubon,
who painted several of his famous bird studies here.
The masterful Gray Plantation is our local affiliate.

CHICKEN ENCHILADAS WITH GREEN SAUCE

SERVES 12

GREEN SAUCE	CHICKEN ENCHILADAS
1 onion, quartered	3 whole chickens, cooked and boned
12 to 14 tomatillos, skins removed	2 teaspoons cumin
2 to 3 whole serrano chiles	Salt to taste
6 garlic cloves	Olive oil
1 bunch fresh cilantro	24 corn tortillas
3 to 4 cups chicken broth	1 (8-ounce) package sliced Swiss
2 cups sour cream or	cheese, cut into strips
plain yogurt	4 cups (16 ounces) shredded
	Monterey Jack cheese

SAUCE

Combine the onion, tomatillos, serrano chiles, garlic and cilantro in a saucepan and cover with the broth. Bring to a boil and reduce the heat. Simmer for 6 to 8 minutes or until the vegetables have softened. Remove from the heat and let cool. Purée the cooled vegetable mixture in a blender. Remove half of the puréed mixture to a bowl and reserve. Add the sour cream to the remaining mixture in the blender and process well.

ENCHILADAS

Cut the chicken into bite-size pieces and season with the cumin and salt. Add olive oil to a skillet to cover the bottom and heat over low heat. Add one tortilla and heat until warm, turning once. Remove the tortilla to a work surface and spread 2 tablespoons chicken over one end of the tortilla. Top with two strips Swiss cheese and cover with 2 tablespoons of the sour cream green sauce.

Roll up the tortilla and place seam side down in a large baking dish. Repeat with the remaining tortillas, chicken, Swiss cheese and sour cream green sauce and arrange in the baking dish. Spread the reserved green sauce over the enchiladas and top with the Monterey Jack cheese. Bake in a preheated 350-degree oven for 25 to 30 minutes or until the cheese is bubbly and the edges are beginning to brown.

QUICK GOURMET CHICKEN PIZZA WITH ARUGULA

SERVES 4

1 garlic and herb flavored rotisserie chicken
1 cup sun-dried tomato pesto
1 (14-ounce) baked Italian pizza shell
2 cups (8-ounces) shredded mozzarella cheese
4 cups loosely-packed arugula, torn into bite-size pieces
1 garlic clove, minced
1 tablespoon extra-virgin olive oil
1 tablespoon white wine vinegar
$1/4$ teaspoon salt
$1/4$ teaspoon pepper

Remove the chicken from the bones and cut into bite-size pieces. Spread the pesto over the pizza shell and top with the chicken. Sprinkle with the cheese. Bake in a preheated 450-degree oven for 8 to 12 minutes or until hot and the cheese is melted. Combine the arugula, garlic, olive oil, vinegar, salt and pepper in a bowl and toss to mix. Spread over the hot pizza and serve immediately.

CHICKEN AND AVOCADO PASTA

SERVES 6 TO 8

4 boneless skinless chicken breasts, cut into strips
Salt and pepper to taste
Tex Joy steak seasoning or
Tony Chachere's Creole seasoning to taste
$1/2$ cup (1 stick) butter or margarine
1 (12-ounce) package tri-color spiral pasta,
cooked al dente and drained
$1/3$ cup olive oil
1 cup ranch salad dressing
1 can pitted small black olives, drained
1 small jar pitted green olives, drained and sliced
3 avocados, sliced

Season the chicken with salt and pepper and season generously with Tex Joy seasoning. Melt the butter in a skillet. Add the chicken and sauté until brown and cooked through. Combine the pasta, olive oil and salad dressing in a serving bowl. Season with Tex Joy seasoning and toss to coat. Add the black olives, green olives, avocados and chicken and toss to mix. Serve immediately or chill for 2 hours before serving.

CORNISH HENS "TO DIE FOR"
SERVES 4

4 Cornish game hens, skinned and cleaned
6 tablespoons Calcasieu seasoning mix (page 163)
1/2 cup all-purpose flour
1 tablespoon lemon pepper
4 slices bacon
1/4 cup canola oil
3 onions, chopped
1 bunch celery, chopped
4 garlic cloves, minced
1 red bell pepper, sliced into rings and halved
1 yellow bell pepper, sliced into rings and halved
1 tablespoon chopped fresh basil
1 tablespoon chopped fresh oregano
1 cup chicken stock
1/4 cup sherry
2 carrots, chopped
2 cups fresh button mushrooms, stems trimmed
1/8 teaspoon saffron
Hot cooked rice

Season the game hens with half of the seasoning mix. Combine the flour and lemon pepper in a large sealable plastic bag. Add two game hens; seal the bag and shake to coat. Remove the game hens and repeat with the two remaining game hens. Season the game hens with the remaining seasoning mix. Wrap one slice of bacon around each game hen, circling each twice with the bacon, at opposite ends of the game hen. Heat the olive oil in a skillet. Add the game hens and brown on all sides. Remove to a plate.

Add the onions, celery, garlic, red bell pepper, yellow bell pepper, basil and oregano to the skillet. Sauté over medium heat until the vegetables begin to brown. Place the game hens, breast side up, on the vegetables in the skillet. Add the stock, sherry, carrots, mushrooms and saffron to the skillet. Cook, covered, for 20 minutes. Reduce the heat to low and stir the vegetables; turn the game hens over. Simmer, covered, for 20 minutes. Stir the vegetables and turn the game hens. Simmer, covered, for 20 minutes longer or until the birds are cooked through. Serve over hot cooked rice.

SPINACH PHYLLO PIE

SERVES 6

1 tablespoon olive oil or vegetable oil
$1/2$ cup chopped onion
1 cup chopped red bell pepper
1 garlic clove, minced
2 (9-ounce) packages frozen chopped spinach,
thawed and squeezed dry
8 ounces cream cheese, softened
$1/2$ cup crumbled feta cheese or
Gorgonzola cheese
2 eggs
1 tablespoon chopped fresh dill weed, or
1 teaspoon dried dill weed
$1/2$ teaspoon salt
$1/2$ teaspoon pepper
8 (9×14-inch) sheets phyllo dough, thawed
2 tablespoons butter or margarine, melted

Heat the olive oil in a skillet over medium-high heat. Add the onion, bell pepper and garlic and sauté until tender-crisp. Remove from the heat and stir in the spinach, cream cheese, feta cheese, eggs, dill weed, salt and pepper. Trim the phyllo dough on a work surface to a 9×12-inch stack and discard the trimmed dough. Cover the dough with waxed paper and then a damp kitchen towel to prevent drying. Remove four sheets of dough and brush each with melted butter. Layer the buttered phyllo dough into a greased 9-inch pie plate, gently pressing into the pie plate and allowing the excess dough to hang over the edge. Spread the spinach mixture evenly over the buttered phyllo dough. Fold the overhanging phyllo dough over the filling. Brush the remaining sheets of phyllo dough with melted butter and layer over the top of the spinach mixture. Tuck the overhanging phyllo dough gently into the pie plate. Cut the pie into six wedges with a sharp knife. Bake in a preheated 375-degree oven until heated through and golden brown. Let stand for 10 minutes before serving.

ASPARAGUS LINGUINI

SERVES 6

1/4 cup finely chopped onion
3 garlic cloves, minced
2 tablespoons light margarine
8 ounces fresh asparagus, trimmed, peeled and sliced diagonally into 1/2-inch pieces
2 tablespoons dry white wine

2 tablespoons fresh lemon juice
5 ounces linguini, cooked al dente and drained
1/4 cup grated Parmesan cheese
3/4 cup (3 ounces) shredded light mozzarella cheese

Sauté the onion and garlic in the margarine in a skillet until tender. Add the asparagus and sauté for 2 minutes. Add the wine and lemon juice and cook for 1 minute, stirring constantly. Remove to a large bowl. Add the hot pasta and Parmesan cheese and toss to mix. Remove to a serving platter and top with the mozzarella cheese.

FRESH TOMATO VERMICELLI

SERVES 4

6 tablespoons olive oil
1 garlic clove, minced
1 1/2 cups chopped, seeded and peeled tomatoes
4 ounces cream cheese, cut into cubes
1 tablespoon wine vinegar

1 teaspoon dried or chopped fresh basil
1/4 teaspoon pepper
8 to 10 ounces vermicelli, cooked al dente and drained
1/2 cup pine nuts
Freshly grated Parmesan cheese

Combine the olive oil, garlic, tomatoes, cream cheese, vinegar, basil and pepper in a large bowl and mix well. Let stand for a few hours. Add the hot pasta and toss to mix. Top with the pine nuts and Parmesan cheese.

You may add chopped black olives and drained canned artichoke hearts to the tomato mixture and top with cooked shrimp.

VODKA AND CREAM PASTA

SERVES 2

1/3 cup vodka
3/4 cup heavy whipping cream
Cayenne pepper to taste
1 (14-ounce) can good-quality plum
tomatoes, chopped
1/2 cup fresh basil, chopped
1/4 cup freshly grated Parmesan cheese
1/4 cup freshly grated Romano cheese
4 ounces penne pasta, cooked
al dente and drained

Add the vodka to a heated skillet. Ignite the vodka with a long match and cook for 20 to 30 seconds or until reduced by half. Whisk in the cream and season with cayenne pepper. Simmer for 5 minutes, whisking frequently. Stir in the tomatoes and basil. Simmer for 5 to 8 minutes. Mix the Parmesan cheese and Romano cheese in a bowl. Add half the cheese mixture and the pasta to the skillet and mix well. Spoon into serving bowls and top with the remaining cheese mixture.

Etouffée
cooked in the "smothered" method;
smothering is similar to braising
but uses lots of onions, celery, and other
vegetables and seasonings. It is then allowed to cook
slowly with a lid on until flavors blend.

BLEND OF THE BAYOUS
Seafood & Game

Known as The Sportsman's Paradise, Louisiana's many lakes, bayous,

and rivers provide a home to numerous species of game, birds, and of course,

fresh seafood. In particular, our coast is home to America's Wetland,

one of the largest and most productive expanses of coastal wetlands in

North America. Here, we work diligently to preserve this natural treasure

as it provides so much for Louisiana and the nation.

As you explore this chapter, you'll discover mouth-watering

delicacies of seafood and game. We hope these prized recipes will

inspire you to prepare a tasty "catch" tonight.

Seafood & Game

Celebration Crawfish Casserole 107 · Gulf Flounder with Crawfish 108

Tropical Baked Fish 108 · Catfish Court Bouillon 109

Redfish Boats 110 · Salmon with Mango Salsa 110 · Smoked Salmon Cheesecake 111

Salmon Marinade 111 · Sautéed Trout 112 · Marinated Tuna Steak 112

Crab Cakes with Lemon-Dill Sauce 113 · Crab Cakes with Tequila Sauce 114

Crab Meat au Gratin 115 · Skinny Crab Enchiladas 115 · Australian Steamed Crabs 116

Outrageous Oyster Bake 116 · Flash-Fried Oysters with Tasso Cream Sauce 117

Cold Cameron Shrimp 118 · "Off the Shelf" Barbecued Shrimp 118

Sizzling Shrimp 119 · Shrimp Newburg 119 · Tomato Coconut Shrimp 122

Pasta and Shrimp with Andouille Sausage 123 · Shrimp Wraps with Pink Sauce 124 · Pink Sauce 124

Weekend Enchiladas 125 · Sautéed Shrimp with Jalapeño Cream Sauce 126

Seafood-Stuffed Eggplant 126 · Scallops with Caramelized Beurre Blanc 127 · Dressed Duck 128

Duck Camp Teal 129 · McNeese Mallard over Rice 130 · Mallard Magic 131

Sitting Duck Marinade 132 · Specklebelly Goose Caribbean Style 132 · Bayou-Style Pheasant 133

Pheasant in Red Wine 133 · Fais do-do Frog Legs 134

Mediterranean Rabbit 135 · Venison Skewers 135

CELEBRATION CRAWFISH CASSEROLE

SERVES 8 TO 10

1 cup chopped celery
1 large white onion, chopped
1 bell pepper, chopped
1 1/2 teaspoons minced garlic
3/4 cup (1 1/2 sticks) butter
1 (10-ounce) can condensed Cheddar cheese soup
1 (10-ounce) can condensed golden mushroom soup
1 teaspoon salt, or to taste
1 teaspoon pepper, or to taste
1 tablespoon Tabasco sauce
1 small bunch parsley, chopped
1 bunch green onions, chopped
2 pounds cooked crawfish tails
2 cups cooked rice
Seasoned bread crumbs

Sauté the celery, white onion, bell pepper and garlic in the butter in a saucepan until tender. Remove from the heat and stir in the Cheddar cheese soup, golden mushroom soup, salt, pepper and Tabasco sauce. Stir in the parsley and green onions. Add the crawfish tails and rice and mix well. Spoon into a nonstick 9×13-inch baking pan or two nonstick 8×8-inch baking pans. Sprinkle with bread crumbs. Bake in a preheated 350-degree oven until heated through and light brown.

This casserole may be made ahead and refrigerated or frozen. Let warm to room temperature before baking.

Make ahead

Cajun Trinity
Celery, onions, and bell peppers

GULF FLOUNDER WITH CRAWFISH

SERVES 4

*Keep a large salt shaker filled
with flour. It's handy and less
messy when dusting pans or
coating chicken. This also works
for confectioners' sugar to shake
out a quick decorative topping.*

1 whole Gulf flounder, skinned and fileted	3 tablespoons extra-virgin olive oil
Tony Chachere's Creole seasoning	3 tablespoons unsalted butter
Italian-style seasoned bread crumbs	1 1/2 cups sliced button mushrooms
3 tablespoons unsalted butter	8 ounces boiled crawfish tails
	Hot cooked rice (optional)

Season the fish filets on both sides with Creole seasoning. Coat the fish
with bread crumbs. Heat 3 tablespoons butter and the olive oil in a large
nonstick skillet. Add the fish and cook for 4 to 5 minutes per side or until the
fish flakes easily; do not overcook. Remove to a platter and keep warm.
Add 3 tablespoons butter to the skillet. Add the mushrooms and sauté for
3 minutes. Add the crawfish tails and sauté until the mushrooms are tender
and all but about 6 tablespoons of liquid has evaporated. Spoon the mushroom
mixture over the fish filets and top with hot cooked rice.

This recipe works well with red snapper or tilapia filets.

TROPICAL BAKED FISH

SERVES 6

*To make clarified butter, melt the
butter slowly. Let it sit for a bit to
separate. Skim off the foam that
rises to the top, and gently pour
the butter off of the milk solids,
which have settled to the bottom.
One stick (8 tablespoons) of butter
will produce about 6 tablespoons
of clarified butter.*

BAKED FISH	TROPICAL FRUIT SAUCE
6 redfish or catfish filets	1/2 cup (1 stick) light butter
5 tablespoons Calcasieu seasoning mix (page 163)	2 cups chopped papayas
	1 cup chopped mango
2 eggs	1 cup chopped pineapple
1 cup skim milk	2 bananas, sliced
1 cup all-purpose flour	1/2 red bell pepper, roasted, peeled and sliced
1/2 cup (1 stick) light butter, clarified	1/2 yellow bell pepper, roasted, peeled and sliced

FISH
Season the filets with the seasoning mix. Whisk the eggs and milk in a shallow
dish. Dredge the fish filets in the flour and then coat in the egg mixture.
Sprinkle lightly with flour. Heat the clarified butter in a nonstick skillet. Add the
fish and sauté until golden brown on both sides. Remove the fish to a baking
dish. Bake in a preheated 350-degree oven until the fish flakes easily.

SAUCE
Melt the butter in a 4-quart saucepan. Add the papayas, mango, pineapple,
bananas, red bell pepper and yellow bell pepper. Cook over medium-low heat
until the fruit is warm and 1-inch of liquid is in the bottom of the saucepan,
stirring occasionally. Place the fish on serving plates. Top with the warm fruit
and drizzle with the fruit liquid.

CATFISH COURT BOUILLON
SERVES 8

3 (5-pound) catfish
8 cups water
4 cups vinegar
1/4 cup salt
2 tablespoons Tony Chachere's
    Creole seasoning
6 tablespoons canola oil
4 cups chopped onions
2 cups chopped bell pepper
2 cups chopped celery
3 carrots, thinly sliced
1/4 cup chopped garlic
2 cups chopped parsley
1 cup dark roux
4 cups boiling water

2 (35-ounce) cans whole tomatoes,
    coarsely chopped
2 (15-ounce) cans tomato sauce
1 (15-ounce) can tomatoes with
    green chiles
6 tablespoons Tony Chachere's
    Creole seasoning
1 (6-ounce) can tomato paste
3 tablespoons Pickapeppa Sauce
1/4 cup hot red pepper sauce
4 bay leaves
2 tablespoons brown sugar
1 cup chopped green onions,
    green portions only

Remove the skin from the catfish and cut into 3-inch thick steaks. Clean and skin the heads. Combine 8 cups water, the vinegar and salt in a large container and stir until the salt is dissolved. Add the catfish steaks and heads and let soak for 1 hour. Drain and rinse the steaks and heads. Season the steaks with 2 tablespoons Creole seasoning and place on a platter. Chill, covered, until ready to use. Set the heads aside.

Heat the canola oil in a 12-inch cast-iron Dutch oven until hot. Add 4 cups onions, the bell pepper, celery, carrots, garlic and parsley and sauté over medium heat until the vegetables are tender and beginning to brown. Add the roux and stir well. Add 4 cups boiling water and bring to a boil. Stir in the tomatoes with liquid, the tomato sauce, tomatoes with green chiles, 6 tablespoons Creole seasoning, the tomato paste, Pickapeppa Sauce, hot sauce and bay leaves. Bring to a boil and stir in the brown sugar. Reduce the heat and add the catfish heads. Simmer for several hours or until very thick, stirring frequently. Remove and discard the catfish heads. Add the catfish steaks and simmer until the fish flakes easily; do not overcook. Remove the bay leaves and stir in the green onions. Serve with hot cooked rice.

Court Bouillon

A Louisiana roux-based fish soup made with delicious herbs and wine

REDFISH BOATS

SERVES 1

1 redfish filet (or other firm fish)
Salt and freshly ground pepper
to taste
Paprika
1 teaspoon chopped fresh oregano
1 tablespoon chopped
fresh rosemary
1 onion, thinly sliced

1 garlic clove, sliced
1/2 red bell pepper, thinly sliced
1/2 yellow bell pepper, thinly sliced
4 pitted green olives, sliced
(optional)
1 teaspoon lime juice
2 tablespoons butter,
cut into pieces

Cover a piece of foil with a piece of parchment paper. Place the fish filet on the center of the paper. Season with salt and pepper and sprinkle with paprika. Sprinkle with the oregano and rosemary. Arrange the onion, garlic, red bell pepper, yellow bell pepper and olives on top. Sprinkle with the lime juice and dot with the butter. Crimp the edges and corners of the paper and foil to make a secure open packet. Grill over hot coals for 20 minutes or in a preheated 350-degree oven for 45 minutes or until the fish flakes easily.

SALMON WITH MANGO SALSA

SERVES 6

3/4 cup diced red onion
3/4 cup diced mango
1/2 cup diced red bell pepper
1/2 cup diced green bell pepper
2 plum tomatoes, cored and diced
1 small jalapeño chile, diced
(optional)

1 bunch of fresh parsley or
cilantro, chopped
Juice of 1 lime
1 tablespoon extra-virgin
olive oil
Salt and pepper to taste
1 (2-pound) salmon filet

Combine the onion, mango, red bell pepper, green bell pepper, tomatoes, jalapeño chile, parsley, lime juice and olive oil and mix well. Season with salt and pepper. Let stand at room temperature for flavors to blend. Season the salmon generously with salt and pepper. Cook, skin side down, in a skillet on a grill or in a baking dish in the oven until almost done. Turn the fish over and cook for 2 minutes or until the fish flakes easily. Remove from the heat to a serving platter and top with the mango salsa.

Whether its banana leaves, grape leaves, or cornhusks, it's an ancient cooking tool that is easy to use, especially with fish. Another method of preparing fish is with its scales left on as it will not stick to the cooking surface. The skin and scales can be easily removed after the fish has been cooked.

Soak fish in milk and Tabasco sauce before cooking... it will remove any fishy taste and mildly season the fish.

SMOKED SALMON CHEESECAKE

SERVES 12 TO 16

1 cup (4 ounces) freshly grated Parmesan cheese
1 cup bread crumbs
1/2 cup (1 stick) unsalted butter, melted
1 tablespoon olive oil
1 cup chopped onion
1/2 cup chopped red bell pepper
1/2 cup chopped green bell pepper
2 to 2 1/2 teaspoons salt
1/8 teaspoon freshly ground pepper
28 ounces cream cheese, softened
4 eggs
1/2 cup heavy cream
1 cup (4 ounces) shredded smoked Gouda cheese
1 pound smoked salmon, chopped
Tabasco sauce to taste (optional)

Combine the Parmesan cheese, bread crumbs and melted butter in a bowl and mix well. Press over the bottom of a 9-inch springform pan. Heat the olive oil in a skillet over high heat. Add the onion, red bell pepper and green bell pepper and sauté for 2 to 3 minutes. Stir in the salt and pepper and remove from the heat. Beat the cream cheese, eggs and cream in a mixing bowl until smooth. Stir in the sautéed vegetables, Gouda cheese, salmon and Tabasco sauce. Pour into the prepared crust. Bake in a preheated 350-degree oven for 1 hour and 20 minutes or until firm. Remove to a wire rack and let cool slightly. Chill until cold. Let warm to room temperature before serving. Loosen from the side of the pan with a sharp knife and remove the side.

SALMON MARINADE

SERVES 4 TO 6

1 1/2 cups extra-virgin olive oil
1/2 cup lemon juice
2 tablespoons soy sauce
2 tablespoons Old Bay seasoning
1 tablespoon minced garlic
1 teaspoon ginger
1 1/2 to 2 pounds salmon

Whisk the olive oil, lemon juice, soy sauce, Old Bay seasoning, garlic and ginger in a bowl. Pour over the salmon in a sealable plastic bag and seal the bag. Chill for 15 minutes to overnight, turning the bag occasionally. Remove the salmon and marinade to a baking dish. Bake in a preheated 350-degree oven for 45 minutes or until the fish flakes easily.

Make ahead

SAUTÉED TROUT

SERVES 6

Substitute Italian-style bread crumbs for flour when frying fish for an extra crunch.

12 speckled trout or redfish filets	2 eggs
Tony Chachere's Creole seasoning or Prudhomme's Seafood Magic to taste	Italian-style bread crumbs
	3 tablespoons unsalted butter
	3 tablespoons extra-virgin
1 cup milk	olive oil

Season the fish generously with Creole seasoning. Whisk the milk and eggs in a shallow dish. Coat the seasoned filets in bread crumbs. Coat in the egg mixture and then coat in bread crumbs again. Heat the butter and olive oil in a large heavy nonstick skillet over medium heat. Add the filets in a single layer. Cook for 3 to 4 minutes per side or until the fish flakes easily; do not overcook. Serve with Lemon Butter Caper Sauce (page 160), Saffron Beurre Blanc (page 160) or your favorite sauce.

MARINATED TUNA STEAK

SERVES 4

When you have a spill in the oven... while the oven is still warm, cover the spill with salt and by morning it will be easy to pop off.

1/2 cup olive oil	4 garlic cloves, minced
1/4 cup red wine vinegar	1 teaspoon dry mustard
1/3 cup soy sauce	1/4 teaspoon pepper
2 tablespoons lemon juice	4 fresh tuna steaks
1 tablespoon Worcestershire sauce	Mixed salad greens (optional)

Whisk the olive oil, vinegar, soy sauce, lemon juice, Worcestershire sauce, garlic, dry mustard and pepper in a bowl. Pour over the tuna steaks in a sealable plastic bag and seal the bag. Chill for 4 hours to overnight, turning the bag occasionally. Remove the tuna and discard the marinade. Grill for 5 to 7 minutes per side or until the fish flakes easily. Serve over salad greens.

Make ahead

CRAB CAKES WITH LEMON-DILL SAUCE
SERVES 8

LEMON-DILL SAUCE
1 cup mayonnaise
$1/4$ cup buttermilk
2 tablespoons chopped
fresh dill weed
1 tablespoon chopped fresh parsley
1 tablespoon grated lemon zest
2 teaspoons fresh lemon juice
1 garlic clove, minced

CRAB CAKES
1 tablespoon butter
$1/4$ cup minced green onions
2 tablespoons finely chopped red
bell pepper

1 garlic clove, minced
3 tablespoons heavy cream
1 tablespoon Dijon mustard
1 egg
$1/2$ teaspoon minced fresh parsley
$1/2$ teaspoon cayenne pepper,
or to taste
$1/2$ cup bread crumbs
1 pound claw or lump crab meat
$1/2$ cup bread crumbs
$1/4$ cup grated Parmesan cheese
2 tablespoons vegetable oil
2 tablespoons butter

SAUCE
Combine the mayonnaise, buttermilk, dill weed, parsley, lemon zest, lemon juice and garlic in a bowl and mix well. Chill, covered, until cold.

CRAB CAKES
Melt 1 tablespoon butter in a heavy skillet over medium heat. Add the green onions, bell pepper and garlic and sauté for 3 minutes or until tender. Remove from the heat and stir in the cream, Dijon mustard, egg, parsley, cayenne pepper and $1/2$ cup bread crumbs. Fold in the crab meat gently. Shape the mixture into eight $1/2$-inch patties. Combine $1/2$ cup bread crumbs and cheese in a shallow dish and mix well. Coat the patties in the bread crumb mixture and place on a platter. Chill, covered, for 2 to 24 hours. Heat the oil and 2 tablespoons butter in a skillet. Add the crab cakes and cook for 3 minutes per side or until golden brown. Serve with a dollop of the sauce.

You may bake the crab cakes in a preheated 400-degree oven for 7 to 10 minutes instead of frying.

Make ahead

CRAB CAKES WITH TEQUILA SAUCE

SERVES 6

Here's an easy way to tell the difference between a male and female blue crab. Males have blue claws, and, like most humans, female blue crabs "paint their fingernails" (i.e., the tips of their claws are "painted" red!)

CREOLE CRAB CAKES
3 tablespoons olive oil
1/3 cup chopped onion
1/4 cup chopped green bell pepper
1/4 teaspoon white pepper
Black pepper to taste
1/4 cup chopped green onions
1 tablespoon minced garlic
1 tablespoon plus 1 teaspoon of your favorite Creole seasoning
2 eggs
2 teaspoons Creole mustard
1/2 cup Italian-style bread crumbs
6 tablespoons coarsely grated Parmesan cheese

8 ounces jumbo lump crab meat
5 tablespoons olive oil

TEQUILA SAUCE
1/4 cup tequila
1 tablespoon fresh lime juice
1 1/2 tablespoons minced onion
1/2 teaspoon minced garlic
1 1/2 tablespoons chopped fresh cilantro
1/4 teaspoon salt
Pepper to taste
2 tablespoons heavy cream
1/4 cup (1/2 stick) unsalted butter

CRAB CAKES
Heat 3 tablespoons olive oil in a large skillet over high heat. Add the onion, bell pepper, white pepper and black pepper and sauté for 1 minute. Add the green onions, garlic and Creole seasoning and sauté for 1 minute. Remove the mixture to a bowl and let cool. Whisk the eggs into the vegetable mixture. Stir in the Creole mustard, bread crumbs and cheese. Fold in the crab meat gently. Shape into patties and place on a baking sheet. Chill, covered, until ready to cook. Heat 5 tablespoons olive oil in a large skillet over high heat. Add the crab cakes and cook until golden brown on both sides.

SAUCE
Combine the tequila, lime juice, onion, garlic, cilantro, salt and pepper in a skillet. Bring to a boil, stirring occasionally. Stir in the cream and simmer for a few minutes. Whisk in the butter and remove from the heat. Spoon the sauce onto serving plates and top with the crab cakes. The sauce may be made without the butter the day before serving. Chill, covered, until almost ready to serve. Bring to a simmer over low heat and whisk in the butter.

Make ahead

CRAB MEAT AU GRATIN
SERVES 6

1 cup finely chopped onion
1 rib celery, finely chopped
1/2 teaspoon chopped fresh
 rosemary (optional)
1/2 cup (1 stick) butter
 or margarine
1/4 cup all-purpose flour
2 cups whipping cream, warmed
2 egg yolks

1 teaspoon salt
1/2 teaspoon black pepper
1/4 teaspoon cayenne pepper
1 cup (4 ounces) grated
 Gruyère cheese
1 pound claw or lump crab meat,
 shells removed
1 cup (4 ounces) grated Gruyère
 cheese

Sauté the onion, celery and rosemary in the butter in a saucepan until tender. Whisk in the flour. Cook over medium heat for 5 minutes, stirring frequently. Stir in the cream gradually. Stir in the egg yolks gradually. Stir in the salt, black pepper and cayenne pepper and cook for 5 minutes, stirring frequently. Add 1 cup cheese and cook until melted, stirring constantly. Fold in the crab meat gently. Spoon into a greased 2 1/2-quart baking dish. Sprinkle with 1 cup cheese. Bake in a preheated 375-degree oven for 10 to 15 minutes or until bubbly.

SKINNY CRAB ENCHILADAS
SERVES 6

1 small onion, chopped
1 small green bell pepper, chopped
4 garlic cloves, minced
1 jalapeño chile, finely chopped
1/2 bunch green onions, chopped
1/4 cup (1/2 stick) butter or
3 tablespoons olive oil
1 tablespoon all-purpose flour
1 tablespoon capers
1 1/2 cups low-fat sour cream

3/4 cup (3 ounces) shredded sharp
 Cheddar cheese or Pepper
 Jack cheese
1 pound jumbo lump crab meat
6 white or whole wheat
 flour tortillas
3/4 cup (3 ounces) shredded sharp
 Cheddar cheese or Pepper
 Jack cheese

Sauté the onion, bell pepper, garlic, jalapeño chile and green onions in the butter in a saucepan until tender. Add the flour and cook for 2 minutes, stirring constantly. Add the capers, sour cream and 3/4 cup cheese and mix well. Remove from the heat and gently fold in the crab meat. Spoon equal portions of the mixture over each tortillas and roll up the tortillas. Arrange seam side down in a baking pan coated with nonstick cooking spray. Sprinkle with 3/4 cup cheese. Place under a broiler until the cheese is melted. Serve immediately.

AUSTRALIAN STEAMED CRABS
SERVES 4

1/4 cup olive oil	1 cup (or more) chardonnay
6 garlic cloves, coarsely chopped	1 cup chicken stock
1 cup coarsely chopped green onions	4 Dungeness crabs, cleaned and halved
1/4 cup coarsely chopped fresh ginger	12 blue crabs, cleaned and halved (optional if Dungeness crabs not available)
3 whole chiles, seeded and coarsely chopped	1/2 cup chopped cilantro
1 teaspoon salt	4 limes
1 tablespoon pepper	

Heat the olive oil in a hot wok. Add the garlic, green onions, ginger, chiles, salt and pepper and stir-fry for a few minutes. Add the chardonnay and bring to a boil. Cook until the wine is reduced by one-third and stir in the stock. Add the Dungeness crabs and blue crabs. Steam, covered, for 12 to 15 minutes, stirring every 5 minutes and adding more wine if needed. Stir in the cilantro. Juice the limes and add the lime juice, lime peels and pulp and stir well.

OUTRAGEOUS OYSTER BAKE
SERVES 8

1 cup olive oil	2 to 3 tablespoons Worcestershire sauce
6 garlic cloves, pressed	1/2 teaspoon cayenne pepper
2 cups oysters, drained	1 teaspoon Italian seasoning
1 cup Italian-style bread crumbs	1/3 cup freshly grated Parmesan cheese
1/4 cup (1/2 stick) butter, cut into small pieces	
Juice of 1 lemon	

Mix the olive oil and garlic in a bowl. Coat the oysters in the olive oil mixture and dredge in the bread crumbs. Arrange the oysters in a buttered shallow baking dish. Dot with the butter and drizzle with the lemon juice and Worcestershire sauce. Sprinkle with the cayenne pepper and Italian seasoning. Top with the cheese. Bake in a preheated 450-degree oven for 15 to 20 minutes.

FLASH-FRIED OYSTERS WITH TASSO CREAM SAUCE

SERVES 4 TO 6

TASSO CREAM SAUCE	OYSTERS
1 1/2 pounds tasso, diced	Cornmeal or seasoned fish fry
1/4 cup (1/2 stick) butter	Cajun seasoning to taste
1 onion, chopped	1 pint drained oysters
4 garlic cloves, crushed	Vegetable oil for frying
1 tablespoon all-purpose flour	Hot cooked angel hair pasta
4 to 6 cups heavy cream	1 bunch green onions, chopped,
	for garnish

SAUCE

Brown the tasso in the butter in a saucepan over medium heat. Add the onion and garlic and sauté until tender. Add the flour and cook for 1 minute or until the roux is light blonde, stirring constantly. Stir in the cream. Simmer over low heat for 5 to 10 minutes, stirring frequently. Keep warm.

OYSTERS

Season the cornmeal with Cajun seasoning in a shallow dish. Dredge the oysters in the seasoned cornmeal. Heat oil in a heavy skillet until hot. Add the oysters and cook until the edges curl. Serve the oysters over pasta and top with the sauce. Garnish with green onions.

Tasso

A twice-smoked, richly seasoned lean pork Cajun specialty that is used primarily as a seasoning and is difficult to find outside of Louisiana

COLD CAMERON SHRIMP

SERVES 8

1 1/2 cups vegetable oil
3/4 cup cider vinegar
2 teaspoons salt
1 teaspoon Worcestershire sauce
1/2 teaspoon sugar
1/4 teaspoon hot red pepper sauce
2 1/2 to 3 pounds small to medium cooked
shrimp, peeled
2 cups thinly sliced sweet onions
5 to 7 bay leaves
1 jar capers with liquid
4 to 5 lemons, thinly sliced

Whisk the oil, vinegar, salt, Worcestershire sauce, sugar and hot sauce in a large bowl. Add the shrimp, onions, bay leaves, capers with liquid and lemons and toss gently to mix. Chill, covered, for 8 hours or longer. Remove the bay leaves and serve.

Make ahead

"OFF THE SHELF" BARBECUED SHRIMP

SERVES 4

1 pound (20-count) fresh peeled shrimp
20 slices jalapeño chiles
10 slices bacon, cut in half
1 bottle of your favorite barbecue sauce

Wrap one shrimp and one jalapeño chile slice in one bacon half slice. Secure with a wooden pick. Repeat using all shrimp, jalapeño chiles and bacon. Arrange in a shallow dish and pour the barbecue sauce evenly over the wrapped shrimp. Chill, covered, for several hours. Remove the shrimp and discard the barbecue sauce. Grill over indirect heat until the shrimp turn pink and the bacon is cooked through.

SIZZLING SHRIMP

SERVES 3 TO 4

4 to 5 tablespoons olive oil
4 garlic cloves, minced
1 teaspoon sweet paprika
1 jalapeño chile, minced
1 tablespoon fresh lemon juice
1 tablespoon dry sherry
Salt and pepper to taste
1 pound fresh deveined peeled shrimp

Whisk the olive oil, garlic, paprika, jalapeño chile, lemon juice and sherry in a bowl. Season with salt and pepper. Add the shrimp and toss to coat. Place two small ovenproof skillets 3 to 4 inches below a preheated broiler and heat for up to 5 minutes. Remove the skillets and divide the shrimp mixture evenly between the two skillets. Broil 3 to 4 inches from the heat source for 4 to 5 minutes or until the shrimp turn pink. Serve immediately with French bread.

SHRIMP NEWBURG

SERVES 8

1 cup chopped onion	1/4 cup all-purpose flour
1 cup chopped bell pepper	2 cups half-and-half, heated
1 cup chopped celery	1/4 cup white wine
1 cup chopped green onions	8 slices American cheese
1/2 cup chopped parsley	Salt and pepper to taste
3 garlic cloves, chopped	16 ounces fettuccini,
1/2 cup (1 stick) butter	cooked al dente and drained
1 pound fresh deveined	
peeled shrimp	

Sauté the onion, bell pepper, celery, green onions, parsley and garlic in the butter in a saucepan for 8 minutes or until tender. Stir in the shrimp and cook until the shrimp turn pink. Add the flour and mix well. Stir in the hot half-and-half, wine and cheese. Season with salt and pepper. Spoon into a baking dish and bake in a preheated 350-degree oven for 15 minutes or until heated through and the cheese is melted. Serve over the hot cooked pasta.

TOMATO COCONUT SHRIMP

SERVES 6

1 1/2 tablespoons vegetable oil
1 onion, chopped
1 1/2 teaspoons brown sugar
1/2 red bell pepper, chopped
2 garlic cloves, chopped
1/4 cup all-purpose flour
1 cup canned whole tomatoes, drained and chopped
1 cup well-mixed canned unsweetened coconut milk
1 cup chicken stock
1/2 teaspoon salt
1/4 teaspoon cayenne pepper
12 ounces fresh peeled shrimp
1/4 cup chopped green onions, green portions only
1/4 cup chopped fresh cilantro
Hot cooked rice
1/2 cup toasted flaked coconut (optional)
1/2 cup toasted slivered almonds (optional)

Heat the oil in a 3-quart saucepan. Add the onion and brown sugar and sauté
until tender. Add the bell pepper and garlic and sauté until tender. Add the
flour and cook for 1 minute, stirring constantly. Stir in the tomatoes, coconut
milk and stock. Cook until thickened, stirring constantly. Simmer for 20 minutes,
stirring frequently. Stir in the salt and cayenne pepper. Add the shrimp and cook
just until the shrimp turn pink. Sprinkle with the green onions and cilantro
and serve over hot cooked rice. Top with the toasted coconut and almonds.

You may cook the rice in leftover coconut milk and stock for added flavor.
You may make this recipe ahead up to adding the shrimp; chill. Reheat before
completing the recipe.

Pasta and Shrimp with Andouille Sausage

Serves 4 to 6

8 ounces andouille sausage
1 pound fresh deveined peeled shrimp
5 tablespoons thinly sliced green onions
3/4 cup sliced fresh mushrooms
2 teaspoons minced fresh garlic
1/4 cup white wine

2 cups heavy cream
1 1/2 tablespoons Creole mustard
1 teaspoon Worcestershire sauce
3 tablespoons (about) freshly grated Parmesan cheese
Salt and pepper to taste
Hot cooked pasta

Cut the sausage into 1/4-inch slices and cut the slices in half. Brown the sausage in a heavy skillet. Add the shrimp, green onions, mushrooms and garlic and sauté until the shrimp turn pink. Remove the shrimp mixture to a bowl. Add the wine to the skillet. Cook until the liquid is reduced by half, scraping any brown bits from the bottom of the pan. Add the cream and cook until the liquid is reduced by one-third, stirring frequently. Stir in the Creole mustard, Worcestershire sauce and cheese and season with salt and pepper. Add the shrimp mixture and cook until heated through, stirring frequently. Serve over hot cooked pasta.

Andouille

Renowned Cajun smoked sausage

SHRIMP WRAPS WITH PINK SAUCE

SERVES 4 TO 6

5 cups water	1 cup baby spinach
1 tablespoon crab boil	1 large avocado, sliced
2 tablespoons Tony Chachere's Creole seasoning	1 cup grape tomatoes, sliced
1 pound fresh deveined peeled shrimp	1/2 small purple onion, sliced
4 to 6 sun-dried tomato-basil or spinach tortillas	1 bunch alfalfa sprouts
	1/2 cup Pink Sauce (below)

Bring the water to a boil in a saucepan. Add the crab boil, Creole seasoning and shrimp. Boil for 2 to 3 minutes or until the shrimp turn pink. Drain and let cool. Lay the tortillas on a work surface. Top each with equal portions of the spinach, avocado, tomatoes, onion, alfalfa sprouts and shrimp. Drizzle with the pink sauce. Roll up the tortillas.

PINK SAUCE

MAKES 3 CUPS

1 large onion, quartered	1 tablespoon water
2 garlic cloves, crushed	1 tablespoon horseradish
1 cup mayonnaise	3 tablespoons lemon juice
1/2 cup extra-light olive oil	1 teaspoon mustard
1/3 cup chili sauce	1 teaspoon pepper
2 tablespoons Worcestershire sauce	1 teaspoon paprika
1/2 cup ketchup	

Purée the onion, garlic, mayonnaise, olive oil, chili sauce, Worcestershire sauce, ketchup, water, horseradish, lemon juice, mustard, pepper and paprika in a blender. Remove to a bowl. Chill, covered, for up to 1 week.

Weekend Enchiladas
Serves 8 to 10

2/3 cup chopped white onion
2 garlic cloves, chopped
1 cup chopped green onions
3/4 cup chopped green bell pepper
3/4 cup chopped red bell pepper
1 (4-ounce) can mild or hot chiles
1 cup (2 sticks) margarine
1 teaspoon oregano
Salt and black pepper to taste
Cayenne pepper to taste
2 cups whipping cream
1 cup sour cream
1 1/4 cups (5 ounces) shredded Monterey Jack cheese
2 pounds fresh peeled shrimp, crawfish tails or
shredded cooked chicken
Vegetable oil
8 to 10 flour tortillas
1 1/4 (5 ounces) cups shredded Monterey Jack cheese

Sauté the white onion, garlic, green onions, green bell pepper, red bell pepper and chiles in the margarine in saucepan for 10 minutes. Stir in the oregano and season with salt, black pepper and cayenne pepper. Add the cream and bring to a boil. Reduce the heat and simmer for 10 minutes. Add the sour cream and whisk for 3 minutes. Add 1 1/4 cups cheese. Cook until the cheese is melted, stirring constantly. Remove from the heat.

Sauté the shrimp in a nonstick skillet for 6 minutes or until the shrimp turn pink. Heat oil in a skillet. Fry the tortillas, one at a time, until crisp. Remove to paper towels to drain. Arrange the whole or broken fried tortillas over the bottom of a 9×13-inch baking dish. Top evenly with half the shrimp and spread with half the cheese sauce. Repeat the layers and sprinkle with 1 1/4 cups cheese. Bake in a preheated 350-degree oven for 15 to 20 minutes.

SAUTÉED SHRIMP WITH JALAPEÑO CREAM SAUCE

SERVES 4

1 onion, julienned
1 green bell pepper, julienned
1 red bell pepper, julienned
1 yellow bell pepper, julienned
4 jalapeño chiles, seeded and sliced
1/4 cup (1/2 stick) unsalted butter
3 garlic cloves, crushed

1/8 teaspoon salt
Freshly ground pepper to taste
1 pound fresh deveined peeled shrimp
1 cup sour cream
Hot cooked pasta or rice

Sauté the onion, green bell pepper, red bell pepper, yellow bell pepper and jalapeño chiles in the butter in a saucepan until tender-crisp. Stir in the garlic and salt and season with pepper. Add the shrimp and sauté until the shrimp turn pink. Stir in the sour cream and cook until heated through. Serve over hot cooked pasta.

SPANISH MOSS

Spanish moss is not a moss at all. It's actually a flowering plant from the bromeliad family. It grows hanging from trees in full or partial sunlight, and it thrives in humid climates—from Virginia all the way to Chile. In years past, doctors prescribed medicines extracted from Spanish moss to treat diabetes, and much later it was used as stuffing for mattresses. Today, we simply enjoy its beauty as it hangs from our mighty oaks.

SEAFOOD-STUFFED EGGPLANT

SERVES 3 TO 4

1 eggplant, halved lengthwise
1/4 cup (1/2 stick) butter
1/4 cup all-purpose flour
1/4 to 1/2 cup milk
2 tablespoons chopped onions
1 to 2 green onions, chopped

2 tablespoons chopped fresh parsley
18 medium peeled cooked shrimp
6 ounces lump crab meat
Bread crumbs
Grated Parmesan cheese

Place the eggplant in a baking pan and add a small amount of water to the pan. Bake in a preheated 375-degree oven for 30 minutes or until tender. Remove to wire rack to cool. Scoop out the pulp onto a cutting board, leaving 1/2-inch shells. Chop the pulp. Melt the butter in a saucepan. Add the flour and cook for a few minutes, stirring constantly. Add the milk and cook until thickened, stirring constantly. Remove from the heat and let cool. Sauté the chopped eggplant pulp, onions, green onions, parsley, shrimp and crab meat in a nonstick skillet until the onions are tender. Fold in the white sauce gently and cook until heated through. Spoon the mixture into the eggplant shells. Sprinkle with bread crumbs and cheese. Place on a baking sheet and bake in a preheated 375-degree oven until the tops are golden brown.

SCALLOPS WITH CARAMELIZED BEURRE BLANC

SERVES 2

CARAMELIZED BEURRE BLANC
1/4 cup fresh lime juice
1/4 cup chardonnay
1/4 cup white wine vinegar
2 shallots, minced
2 garlic cloves, pressed
6 tablespoons unsalted butter, cut into 12 slices
1 piece crystallized ginger, minced

SCALLOPS
12 large scallops
1/4 cup soy sauce
2 teaspoons Prudhomme's Seafood Magic
1/4 cup peanut oil

SAUCE
Combine the lime juice, chardonnay and vinegar in a saucepan. Bring to a boil over high heat. Stir in the shallots and garlic and cook until the liquid has evaporated and the vegetables are brown and caramelized. Remove from the heat and immediately whisk in two slices of the butter. Continue adding the butter, one slice at a time. Cook until the butter melts before adding more, whisking constantly. Whisk in the ginger and keep warm.

SCALLOPS
Coat the scallops with the soy sauce in a bowl and let stand for 5 to 10 minutes. Remove the scallops and season on both sides with the Seafood Magic seasoning. Heat a skillet over high heat. Add the peanut oil and heat for 3 minutes or until very hot. Add the scallops in a single layer. Cook for 2 to 3 minutes per side or until brown and caramelized on the top and bottom and just cooked through. Remove to serving plates and top with the sauce.

BIRD WATCHING
An important draw to Southwest Louisiana is bird watching. A number of migratory birds from the North and South American hemispheres, including an abundance of rare species, traverse South Louisiana annually. This creates a spectacle that awes visitors from around the nation.

DRESSED DUCK
SERVES 4 TO 6

4 to 6 teal ducks, cleaned, rinsed and patted dry
Tony Chachere's Creole seasoning to taste
Salt and pepper to taste
4 apples, cored and sliced
4 onions, quartered
1 rib celery, cut into thirds lengthwise and then
into 4-inch pieces
1/4 cup (or more) vegetable oil
1 to 2 cups red wine
2 cups cooked rice

Season the outside and cavity of the ducks with Creole seasoning, salt and
pepper. Place equal portions of some of the apples, some of the onions, and
some of the celery in each of the duck cavities to stuff fully. Heat the oil in
a large heavy saucepan. Add the ducks and brown on all sides. Remove to a
platter. Rinse the saucepan twice but do not scrape the bottom. Return the
ducks to the saucepan. Add water to come halfway up the sides of the pan. Add
the wine and remaining apples, onions and celery. Simmer for 2 to 3 hours
or until the liquid is reduced to 1 inch and the ducks are cooked through.
Remove the ducks and keep warm. Add the rice to the saucepan and stir
gently. Simmer, covered, until most of the liquid has evaporated; do not stir.
Add water if the rice becomes too dry while simmering.

Canard

Duck, which continues to inspire local recipes

DUCK CAMP TEAL
SERVES 4

4 teal ducks, cleaned, rinsed and patted dry
4 to 6 garlic cloves, sliced
4 teaspoons Calcasieu seasoning mix (page 163)
4 green onions, sliced
4 slices bacon, cut in half
1/4 cup Calcasieu seasoning mix (page 163)
2 tablespoons lemon pepper

All-purpose flour for dredging
1/4 cup canola oil
1/4 cup white wine
1 yellow onion, sliced
4 garlic cloves, minced
1 red bell pepper, sliced
1/2 green bell pepper, sliced
1/2 bunch flat-leaf parsley, minced
Hot cooked rice

Make an incision along the breast bone the length of each duck with a sharp knife. Open the incision between the breast bone and both sides of the meat with your finger. Insert garlic slices in each side, using half the garlic slices. Sprinkle 1/2 teaspoon seasoning mix in each side. Insert the green onion slices in each side and add one-half bacon slice to each side. Insert the remaining garlic cloves in each side. Rub the outside of the ducks with 1/4 cup seasoning mix and the lemon pepper. Dredge the ducks in flour and shake off any excess. Heat the canola oil in a cast-iron Dutch oven over medium heat. Add the ducks, breast side down, and sear the breast side. Reduce the heat to medium-low and cook until the ducks are well-browned on all sides. Remove the ducks to a platter.

Add the wine to the pan and cook, scraping any brown bits from the bottom of the pan. Add the onion, garlic, red bell pepper, green bell pepper and parsley and sauté over medium heat until the onions are tender. Reduce the heat to medium-low and add the ducks, breast side down. Add 2 tablespoons water and simmer, covered, for 30 minutes. Stir occasionally and add water 1 tablespoon at a time, if needed to keep the ducks moist. Turn the ducks over and simmer, covered, for 1 hour. Stir occasionally, adding water 1 tablespoon at a time, if needed. Turn the ducks over and simmer, covered, for 30 minutes. Stir occasionally and add water 1 tablespoon at a time if needed. Turn the ducks over and simmer, covered, until very tender and cooked through. Adjust seasonings to taste. Serve over hot cooked rice.

SPORTSMAN'S PARADISE
From duck camps to fishing rodeos, South Louisiana is the Sportsmen's Paradise. When we think of hunting and fishing, we immediately fantasize about the irresistible aroma of a duck gumbo cooking or the incredible scent of "just caught" speckled trout sizzling over the fire. Now that's paradise!

MᴄNᴇᴇsᴇ Mᴀʟʟᴀʀᴅ ᴏᴠᴇʀ Rɪᴄᴇ

Sᴇʀᴠᴇs 2

1 mallard duck	2 tablespoons butter
2 cups chicken broth	2 tablespoons all-purpose flour
1/2 cup dry sherry	Tabasco sauce to taste
1/2 teaspoon pepper	Salt to taste
1 bay leaf	All-purpose flour for dredging
1 cup sliced onions	Pepper to taste
1 cup sliced fresh mushrooms	Cooked rice
Butter for sautéing	Currant jelly

Remove the duck breasts with a sharp knife, keeping each breast in one piece. Place the duck breasts in a shallow dish and discard the remainder of the duck. Mix the broth, sherry, pepper and bay leaf in a bowl pour over the duck. Chill, covered, for 4 hours to overnight.

Sauté the onions and mushrooms in butter in a skillet until tender. Melt 2 tablespoons butter in a saucepan and stir in the flour. Cook until the roux is light brown, stirring constantly. Remove from the heat. Remove the duck from the marinade and pat dry. Remove the bay leaf and reserve the marinade. Rub the duck skin with Tabasco sauce and salt and dust with flour. Brown the duck in butter in a cast-iron skillet. Remove the duck to a shallow baking dish.

Stir the roux into the skillet. Whisk in the reserved marinade. Cook over low heat for 5 minutes, stirring frequently. Stir in the onions and mushrooms. Adjust the seasonings to taste. Pour over the duck in the baking dish and cover with foil. Bake in a preheated 325-degree oven for 2 hours. Remove the foil and bake for 1 hour longer or until the duck is tender, cooked through, and brown and the sauce is thickened. Serve over rice with currant jelly on the side.

Roux

A flour and oil mixture that forms the foundation for gumbo and other staples of Louisiana cooking.

MALLARD MAGIC

SERVES 2

2 fresh mallard ducks, cleaned,
rinsed and patted dry
1 (12-ounce) jar Cajun Injector for chicken and
turkey with injector
1/2 cup plus 2 tablespoons Calcasieu
seasoning mix (page 163)
All-purpose flour for dredging
1/3 cup canola oil
3 tablespoons all-purpose flour
1 yellow onion, chopped
5 garlic cloves, minced
1/2 cup good-quality red wine
1/4 cup water
12 slices bacon, cut in half
1 cup chopped green onions,
green portions only

Inject each duck breast with Cajun Injector, using one insert hole and fanning out to spread the seasoning, refilling the injector as needed. Inject each leg and at the base of each wing once. Rub the outside of the ducks with the seasoning mix. Dredge the ducks in flour and shake off any excess. Heat the canola oil in a cast-iron Dutch oven over medium heat. Add the ducks and brown on all sides. Remove the ducks to a platter.

Scrape any brown bits from the bottom and sides of the pan. Add the 3 tablespoons flour and cook until the roux is medium-dark brown, stirring constantly. Add the onion and garlic and sauté until tender. Stir in the wine and water. Add the ducks, breast side up, and arrange the bacon slices over the ducks. Reduce the heat and cover. Simmer for 1 hour, stirring occasionally and adding up to 1/4 cup water if needed to prevent the sauce becoming too thick. Add the green onions and cook until the ducks are very tender and cooked through. Serve with rice.

AMERICA'S WETLAND
The land extending along Louisiana's coast is known as America's Wetland and is one of the largest and most productive expanses of coastal wetlands in the North America. This valuable landscape is unfortunately disappearing at a rate of 25 square miles per year. In the largest public awareness initiative in its history, Louisiana is leading **America's Wetland: Campaign to Save Coastal Louisiana***. This effort is raising awareness of the impact that wetland loss has on America and is diligently working to increase support for efforts to conserve and save coastal Louisiana. All Americans should be aware of this crisis. For more information, or to see how you can help, please go to www.americaswetland.com.*

SITTING DUCK MARINADE
SERVES 2

1 duck breast	1/2 cup sesame oil
Pepper to taste	1 garlic clove, chopped
MSG to taste	1/2 teaspoon ginger
3/4 cup sugar	1 bunch green onions, chopped
1/2 cup soy sauce	2 tablespoons sesame seeds

Season the duck with pepper and MSG and place in a shallow dish. Whisk the sugar, soy sauce, sesame oil, garlic, ginger, green onions and sesame seeds in a bowl. Pour over the duck. Chill, covered, for 2 to 48 hours, turning occasionally. Remove the duck and discard the marinade. Grill the duck or sauté in a skillet until tender and cooked through.

 Make ahead

SPECKLEBELLY GOOSE CARIBBEAN STYLE
SERVES 10 TO 12

3 specklebelly geese, cleaned, rinsed and patted dry	1 cup (2 sticks) unsalted butter, cut into slices
Tony Chachere's Creole seasoning to taste, or salt and pepper to taste	2 red bell peppers, sliced
	2 green bell peppers, sliced
	2 yellow bell peppers, sliced
1 cup cider vinegar	5 oranges, sliced
4 cups packed brown sugar	1 (20-ounce) can pineapple
1 cup red wine	chunks, drained
1 (12-ounce) can cola	

Rub the outside of the geese with Creole seasoning and place in a roasting pan. Combine the vinegar and brown sugar in a bowl and mix well. Pour over the geese. Pour the wine and cola into the pan around the geese. Arrange the butter slices over the geese and top with the red bell peppers, green bell peppers and yellow bell peppers. Arrange the orange slices over the bell peppers and top with the pineapple. Roast, covered, in a preheated 350-degree oven for 4 to 6 hours or until the geese are very tender and cooked through. Serve with brown rice and cooked green beans.

Bayou-Style Pheasant

Serves 4

1 deep covered clay cooking pot
2 whole pheasants, cleaned, rinsed and patted dry
1 (12-ounce) jar Cajun Injector for chicken and turkey with injector
Calcasieu seasoning mix (page 163)
1/2 cup (1 stick) butter, clarified
8 slices bacon
1/3 cup cognac
1 cup chicken stock
2 cups fresh pearl onions
2 cups fresh mushrooms, stems trimmed
2 cups baby carrots
1 tablespoon cornstarch
1 tablespoon cold water
Hot cooked rice

Soak the clay pot in water for several hours; drain. Inject the pheasants with the Cajun Injector. Season generously with seasoning mix. Heat the butter in a skillet over high heat. Add the pheasants and brown on all sides. Remove the pheasants to the clay pot, breast side up. Sprinkle with seasoning mix. Arrange the bacon slices over the pheasants. Add the cognac, stock, onions, mushrooms and carrots to the pot. Bake, covered, in a preheated 350-degree oven for 1 1/2 hours or until the pheasants are tender. Remove the vegetables with a slotted spoon to a serving platter. Remove the pheasants to a cutting board and cut into serving pieces. Add the pheasant to the vegetables and keep warm. Remove the cooking liquid to a saucepan and heat until hot. Dissolve the cornstarch in the water in a bowl. Stir into the cooking liquid. Cook over high heat until thickened, stirring constantly. Serve over the pheasant, vegetables and rice.

Pheasant in Red Wine

Serves 4

1 pheasant, cut up
Salt and pepper to taste
All-purpose flour for dredging
2 tablespoons butter
2 tablespoons vegetable oil
1 apple, cored and cut into 8 slices
1/2 cup red wine
1 cup chicken stock
1/2 cup cream or sour cream

Season the pheasant with salt and pepper and dredge in flour. Heat the butter and oil in a skillet. Add the pheasant and brown quickly on all sides. Remove to a roasting pan and arrange the apple slices around the edge of the pan. Add the wine to the skillet and cook, scraping any brown bits from the bottom of the pan. Add the stock and cook for 5 minutes, stirring frequently. Pour over the pheasant. Cook, covered, in a preheated 375-degree oven for 30 minutes. Reduce the heat to 350 degrees and cook for 1 hour or until the pheasant is tender. Remove the pheasant with a slotted spoon to a serving platter and let stand for 10 minutes. Add the cream to the roasting pan and simmer for a few minutes, stirring frequently. Pour over the pheasant and serve. Quail may be substituted, if desired.

FAIS DO-DO FROG LEGS
SERVES 2

FAIS DO-DO

*Fais do-do is an expression
meaning "make sleep," from
the French words "faire" and
"dormir." In the Louisiana French
music tradition, a fais do-do
provides the title and lyrics for
lullabies. Later it also came to be
used as the name for community
dances. It is believed that at the
old-time house dances and dance
halls, the children slept in a side
room while the adults danced the
night away in the main room.*

6 pair cleaned frog legs
2 tablespoons Prudhomme's Seafood Magic
1 yellow onion, minced
1/2 cup (1 stick) unsalted butter, cut up
3 garlic cloves, minced
2/3 cup tomato sauce
1 cup sliced mushrooms
2 tablespoons chopped flat-leaf parsley
6 birdseye chiles, minced
1 large pinch of saffron threads
1/4 cup chopped fresh sweet basil
1/4 teaspoon minced fresh oregano
1/4 teaspoon minced fresh thyme
8 fresh rosemary leaves, minced
1 tablespoon herbes de Provence
1 teaspoon sea salt
1 cup all-purpose flour
1 tablespoon Prudhomme's Seafood Magic
1/2 teaspoon sea salt
1 cup whipping cream
3/4 cup extra-virgin olive oil
Hot cooked rice

Sprinkle the frog legs with 2 tablespoons Seafood Magic seasoning and place
in a sealable plastic bag. Seal the bag and chill for 1 hour. Sauté the onion in
the butter in a saucepan until tender. Stir in the garlic, tomato sauce, mushrooms,
parsley, birdseye chiles, saffron, basil, oregano, thyme, rosemary, herbes
de Provence and 1 teaspoon salt. Simmer for 10 minutes, stirring frequently;
keep warm.

Mix the flour, 1 tablespoon Seafood Magic seasoning and 1/2 teaspoon salt
in a shallow dish. Pour the cream into a bowl. Coat the frog legs in the cream
and dredge in the flour mixture. Heat the olive oil in a skillet. Add the frog legs
and sauté until well browned. Remove the frog legs to a shallow baking dish
and pour the sauce evenly over the frog legs. Bake in a preheated 350-degree
oven for 30 minutes or until cooked through. Adjust the seasonings to taste.
Serve over rice with your favorite cooked vegetable on the side.

MEDITERRANEAN RABBIT
SERVES 4

2 whole young farm-raised rabbits, cut up
Calcasieu seasoning mix (page 163)
Whole wheat flour for dredging
1/2 cup (1 stick) unsalted butter, clarified
5 tablespoons extra-virgin olive oil
2 yellow onions, chopped
6 garlic cloves, minced
2 teaspoons minced fresh thyme
1 teaspoon minced fresh oregano
2 tablespoons minced fresh sweet basil
1 large pinch of saffron threads
1 cup chardonnay
1 cup fat-free half-and-half
2 cups fat-free chicken stock
2 teaspoons cornstarch
1 tablespoon cold water
Hot cooked linguini
Freshly grated Parmigiano-Reggiano cheese

Season the rabbit generously with seasoning mix and dredge in whole wheat flour. Heat the clarified butter and olive oil in a large Dutch oven. Add the rabbit and brown on all sides. Remove with a slotted spoon to a platter. Add the onions and garlic to the Dutch oven and sauté until brown. Add the thyme, oregano and basil and cook for 3 minutes, stirring frequently. Stir in the saffron, chardonnay, half-and-half and stock. Bring to a boil and add the rabbit. Return to a boil and reduce the heat to medium-low. Cook, covered, for 1 hour or until the rabbit is tender and cooked through. Remove the rabbit with a slotted spoon to a platter. Bring the sauce to a boil. Dissolve the cornstarch in the water in a bowl and stir into the sauce. Cook until thickened, stirring frequently. Adjust the seasonings to taste and add the rabbit. Cook, covered, until the rabbit is heated through. Serve over hot pasta and top with cheese.

VENISON SKEWERS
MAKES A VARIABLE AMOUNT

Canned jalapeño chiles, split
Venison back strap, cut into 1/2-inch slices
Bacon slices
Salt and pepper to taste
Barbecue sauce
Worcestershire sauce
Onion slices
Bell pepper pieces
Cherry tomatoes

Place one split jalapeño chile between two venison slices. Wrap one bacon slice around the venison and secure with wooden picks. Repeat using all the venison, jalapeño chiles and bacon. Place in a shallow dish and season with salt and pepper. Top with barbecue sauce and Worcestershire sauce. Chill, covered, for a few hours. Remove the venison and discard the marinade. Thread the venison alternately with onions, bell peppers and cherry tomatoes onto skewers. Grill over hot coals to medium-rare. Do not overcook or the venison will be dry and tough.

SOUTHERN SIDES
Side Dishes

In Southwest Louisiana, we are serious about side dishes.

Cherished for the color, character, and flavor they add to meals,

sides are where our culinary training begins. Mothers teach their

children to cook starting with these tantalizing dishes.

Familiar and comfortable, these savory traditions are carried on, bayou style,

one family at a time. Additionally, you'll discover our great fortune, as the

land on which we live produces many of the foundations for our recipes.

This chapter brings a personal touch that gives us great pride, as scrumptious

side dishes and luscious sauces turn simple meals into something quite special.

Here, there is no such thing as sitting quietly . . . on the side!

Side Dishes

Garlicky Sesame Asparagus 139 · Italian Green Beans 139

Pesto Green Beans 140 · Maque Choux 140 · Jalapeño Corn Soufflé 141

Farmers' Market Mirlitons 141 · Okra Patties 142 · House Party Vidalia Onions 142

Boursin Potato Cakes 143 · German Potato Salad 144 · Sweet Potato Balls 144

Sweet Potatoes with Maple-Jalapeño Sour Cream 145 · Spinach Mushroom "Cheeserole" 146

Ranch Squash 147 · Zucchini with Basil Sauce 147

Stuffed Zucchini with Béchamel Sauce 148 · Béchamel Sauce 149

Coffee-Kissed Baked Bananas 149 · Pineapple Casserole 152 · Brown Sugar Bacon 152

Oysters Rockefeller Casserole 153 · Oyster Bread Dressing 153 · Hearty Corn Bread Dressing 154

Grits on Fire 155 · Goat Cheese Grits 155 · Three-Cheese Macaroni with Cheddar Sauce 156

Bangkok Crab Fried Rice 157 · Rice with an Attitude 157 · 411 Sauce 158

White Barbecue Chicken Sauce 158 · Old World Sweet-and-Sour Sauce 159

Saffron Beurre Blanc 160 · Lemon Butter Caper Sauce 160 · Saffron Butter Cream Sauce 161

Classic Béarnaise Sauce 162 · Calcasieu Seasoning Mix 163

GARLICKY SESAME ASPARAGUS

SERVES 4

1 pound fresh asparagus, trimmed
¹/4 cup water
¹/4 cup rice vinegar
3 tablespoons soy sauce
2 teaspoons dark sesame oil
2 garlic cloves, crushed
Sesame seeds (optional)

Arrange the asparagus in a 7×11-inch microwave-safe baking dish and add the water. Microwave on High for 3 minutes or until tender; drain. Mix the vinegar, soy sauce, sesame oil and garlic in a bowl. Pour over the asparagus and turn to coat. Chill, covered, for 1 hour to overnight. Sprinkle with the sesame seeds and serve chilled or at room temperature.

Make ahead

ITALIAN GREEN BEANS

SERVES 4

1 pound beef or pork sausage links,
cut into bite-size pieces
1 cup water
1 to 2 pounds fresh green beans,
trimmed and cut into thirds
4 to 8 small new potatoes
1 can tomato sauce
2 cups water
¹/2 teaspoon salt
¹/2 teaspoon pepper

Brown the sausage in a large saucepan over medium heat and drain off any excess fat. Add 1 cup water to the saucepan and scrape any brown bits from the bottom of the pan. Add the green beans, potatoes, tomato sauce, 2 cups water, salt and pepper and mix well. Bring to a boil and reduce the heat. Simmer, partially covered, for 30 to 45 minutes or until the sauce is thickened and the green beans are tender, stirring occasionally. To serve as an entrée, add more sausage and potatoes.

PESTO GREEN BEANS

SERVES 8

2 pounds fresh green beans, trimmed
$1/4$ cup ($1/2$ stick) butter or margarine
2 garlic cloves, pressed
1 teaspoon dried pesto seasoning
$1/2$ teaspoon salt

Place the green beans in a steamer basket over boiling water in a large saucepan. Steam, covered, for 6 minutes or until tender-crisp.

Melt the butter in a large skillet over medium-low heat and stir in the garlic, pesto seasoning and salt. Sauté for 1 minute and mix in the green beans. Sauté for 2 minutes or until heated through. Serve immediately.

MAQUE CHOUX

SERVES 4

6 ears fresh corn
2 tablespoons butter
$1/2$ cup chopped yellow onion
$1/2$ cup chopped green bell pepper
$1/2$ (10-ounce) can tomatoes with green chiles
$1/4$ teaspoon salt
Dash of Tabasco sauce

Hold the ears of corn upright in a bowl and run the tip of a small knife down the kernels and then scrape the kernels from the cob into the bowl. Melt the butter in a saucepan over medium heat. Add the onion and bell pepper and reduce the heat to medium-low. Cook for 15 minutes. Stir in the corn, tomatoes with green chiles, salt and Tabasco sauce; reduce the heat. Simmer for 10 to 15 minutes and serve hot.

Maque Choux

A South Louisiana dish made of sweet corn, smothered onions, butter, garlic and tomato. It is traditionally fried.

JALAPEÑO CORN SOUFFLÉ

SERVES 12

1 cup yellow cornmeal	1 large onion, diced
1 tablespoon sugar	3 cups (12 ounces) shredded
1½ teaspoons baking powder	Cheddar cheese
1 teaspoon salt	2 jalapeño chiles, seeded
2 eggs, beaten	and minced
½ cup bacon drippings	4 to 5 garlic cloves, pressed
1 (14-ounce) can cream-style corn	1 tablespoon Tabasco sauce

Combine the cornmeal, sugar, baking powder and salt in a large bowl and mix
well. Add the eggs, bacon drippings, corn, onion, cheese, jalapeño chiles, garlic
and Tabasco sauce and mix well. Spoon into a greased 9×12-inch baking dish.
Bake in a preheated 400-degree oven for 40 minutes.

*Season fresh corn on the cob
with olive oil and your favorite
spices—then throw it on the
grill for an extra special treat!*

FARMERS' MARKET MIRLITONS

SERVES 6 TO 8

4 to 5 mirlitons	½ bell pepper, chopped
3 to 4 slices bacon	1 cup (or more) bread crumbs
1 pound ground beef	Salt and pepper to taste
1 large onion, chopped	

Cook the mirlitons in a saucepan of boiling water until tender; drain and
let cool. Cut the mirlitons in half lengthwise. Scoop the pulp into a bowl,
leaving ½-inch shells, and mash the pulp. Cook the bacon in a skillet until crisp;
drain on paper towels and crumble. Drain most of the drippings from
the skillet. Add the ground beef, onion and bell pepper to the skillet. Cook
until the ground beef is crumbly; drain. Add the ground beef mixture, bread
crumbs and crumbled bacon to the mirliton pulp. Season with salt and pepper
and mix well, adding more bread crumbs if needed. Spoon the mixture into
the mirliton shells. Bake in a preheated 350-degree oven for 30 minutes or until
heated through.

   You may use chopped ham, crawfish, crab meat or shrimp instead of the
ground beef.

*Mirlitons, also known as vegetable
pears, originally came from the
Aztec and Mayan civilizations.
The mirliton, which is grown
on a vine, is a very common
vegetable in South Louisiana.
It has a very mild flavor and is
prone to absorbing the flavors
of other foods with which it
is cooked.*

OKRA PATTIES

MAKES ABOUT 12

Ground okra seeds were used as a coffee substitute by southerners during the American Civil War.

½ cup all-purpose flour
½ cup cornmeal
1 teaspoon baking powder
1 egg
1 pound cut okra
½ cup chopped onion
1 teaspoon salt
¼ teaspoon pepper
½ cup water
Vegetable oil for frying

Sift the flour, cornmeal and baking powder together. Beat the egg in a bowl. Stir in the okra, onion, salt, pepper and water. Add the dry ingredients and mix well. Drop by spoonfuls into hot oil in a skillet. Cook over medium heat until brown on both sides. Remove to paper towels to drain.

HOUSE PARTY VIDALIA ONIONS

SERVES 12

Sprinkle dry powdered milk onto overcooked potatoes to make them fluffy.

8 Vidalia onions, cut into wedges
¼ cup (½ stick) butter
1 cup cooked rice
1 cup (4 ounces) shredded Swiss cheese
1 cup half-and-half
Salt and white pepper to taste

Sauté the onions in the butter in a skillet until translucent. Remove to a bowl and add the rice, cheese and half-and-half. Season with salt and white pepper and mix well. Spoon into a 9×12-inch baking dish. Bake in a preheated 350-degree oven for 30 to 40 minutes or until golden brown.

BOURSIN POTATO CAKES

SERVES 4

1 russet potato, peeled
1 tablespoon vegetable oil
Coarse salt and freshly ground pepper
2 1/2 ounces boursin cheese, crumbled
3 green onions, chopped
1 tablespoon vegetable oil

Grate the potato coarsely onto a kitchen towel. Gather the edges of the towel
and squeeze out the moisture from the potato. Heat 1 tablespoon oil in a
nonstick skillet over medium heat. Spread half the grated potato onto the
bottom of the skillet and press with a metal spatula to make a solid layer.
Season with salt and pepper. Sprinkle the cheese and green onions over the
potato cake, leaving a 1/2-inch border. Spread the remaining grated potato
over the top and press with a metal spatula to make a solid layer. Cook for
10 minutes or until crisp and golden brown on the bottom. Place a baking
sheet over the skillet and carefully invert the potato cake onto the baking sheet.
Add 1 tablespoon oil to the skillet and heat until hot. Slide the potato cake,
browned side up, into the skillet. Cook until crisp and golden brown on the
bottom. Remove the potato cake to a serving plate. Cut into eight wedges
and serve immediately.

   This can be made up to 2 hours ahead. Place on a baking sheet and let stand
at room temperature. Warm in a preheated 350-degree oven for 15 minutes
or until crisp.

Make ahead

Pirogue

a dugout canoe made from a single tree trunk.
This flat-bottomed boat is used to
navigate the shallow waters of the many marshes
and bayous of Louisiana.

GERMAN POTATO SALAD
SERVES 6

6 large russet potatoes
1 pound lean bacon, cut crosswise into thin strips
1 large yellow onion, thinly sliced
1/3 cup cider vinegar
1 1/2 cups water
Salt and pepper to taste

Cook the potatoes in a saucepan of boiling salted water until tender. Drain and
let cool. Peel the potatoes and cut into slices. Cook the bacon in a heavy
saucepan until crisp. Remove the bacon with a slotted spoon to paper towels
to drain. Add the onion to the bacon drippings in the saucepan and sauté until
light brown. Mix the vinegar and water in a 2-cup measuring cup. Add to the
onions and mix well. Add the crumbled bacon and sliced potatoes. Season
with salt and pepper and mix well. Simmer until the liquid is reduced. Remove
from the heat and let stand for 1 hour before serving. Reheat before serving.

SWEET POTATO BALLS
SERVES 12

2 large cans yams, drained
3/4 cup granulated sugar
1 cup cornflakes, crushed
1 tablespoon butter, softened
1/2 cup (1 stick) butter, melted
2/3 cup packed brown sugar
4 dashes of cinnamon
2/3 cup pecans, chopped

Beat the yams, granulated sugar, cornflakes and 1 tablespoon butter in a mixing
bowl until well combined. Shape into small balls and arrange in a baking dish.
Make an indentation in each ball with the back of a small spoon. Mix 1/2 cup
butter, the brown sugar and cinnamon in a bowl. Add the pecans and mix well.
Fill each indentation in the balls with the pecan mixture. Bake in a preheated
350-degree oven for 10 minutes or until heated through.

Sweet Potatoes with Maple-Jalapeño Sour Cream

Serves 4

¹/₂ cup sour cream or plain yogurt
1 tablespoon maple syrup
2 teaspoons minced seeded jalapeño chiles
1 teaspoon fresh lime juice
Salt to taste
Tabasco sauce to taste
4 sweet potatoes
Vegetable oil
Bacon bits
Chopped green onions

Combine the sour cream, maple syrup, jalapeño chiles and lime juice in a bowl.
Season with salt and Tabasco sauce and mix well. Chill until cold. Rub the sweet
potatoes with oil and sprinkle with salt. Bake directly on a rack in a preheated
450-degree oven for 40 to 45 minutes or until tender. Slice the potatoes in half
lengthwise and serve with the maple-jalapeño sour cream, bacon bits and
green onions.

Lache pas la patate

Don't drop the hot potato

Spinach Mushroom "Cheeserole"

Serves 12

6 bags fresh baby spinach
1 large onion, coarsely chopped
1 large package fresh mushrooms, sliced
3 tablespoons butter
2 cups heavy whipping cream
8 ounces cream cheese
2 cups (8 ounces) shredded hot pepper cheese
Salt and white pepper to taste
Tabasco sauce to taste
Fine cracker crumbs
1 tablespoon butter, cut into pieces
1 cup (4 ounces) shredded Gruyère cheese

Sauté the spinach in a nonstick skillet just until tender; drain. Squeeze the spinach dry and chop. Sauté the onion and mushrooms in 3 tablespoons butter in a skillet until tender. Add the cream and cream cheese and cook until the cream cheese is melted, stirring frequently. Stir in the hot pepper cheese and season with salt, pepper and Tabasco sauce. Fold in the chopped spinach and adjust the seasonings to taste. Spoon into a buttered 9×13-inch baking dish. Top with cracker crumbs and dot with 1 tablespoon butter. Bake in a preheated 350-degree oven for 30 minutes. Sprinkle with the Gruyère cheese and bake just until the cheese is melted. Serve immediately.

Champignon
Mushrooms, both wild and cultivated

Ranch Squash
Serves 12

4 cups sliced squash
2 onions, chopped
1 chicken bouillon cube
4 eggs
2 cups mayonnaise
1 envelope ranch salad dressing mix

2 cups (8 ounces) shredded sharp Cheddar cheese
1 sleeve butter crackers, crushed
Crushed butter crackers for topping
1 pound bacon, crisp-cooked and crumbled (optional)

Sauté the squash, onions and bouillon cube in a skillet until the vegetables are tender; drain. Beat the eggs in a mixing bowl. Add the mayonnaise and salad dressing mix and beat well. Stir in the squash mixture, cheese and one sleeve crushed crackers. Spoon into a 9×13-inch baking dish. Top with additional crushed crackers and sprinkle with the bacon. Bake in a preheated 350-degree oven for 30 minutes.

Zucchini with Basil Sauce
Serves 6

3 tablespoons butter
3 tablespoons olive oil
2 pounds zucchini, julienned
2 teaspoons all-purpose flour
1/3 cup milk
2/3 cup chopped fresh basil, or 2 tablespoons dried basil

Salt and pepper to taste
1 egg yolk, lightly beaten
1/2 cup (2 ounces) freshly grated Parmesan cheese
1/4 cup freshly grated Romano cheese

Heat the butter and olive oil in a skillet until hot; do not let brown. Add the zucchini and sauté until tender-crisp. Whisk the flour and milk in a bowl and stir into the zucchini. Stir in the basil and season with salt and pepper. Remove from the heat and quickly stir in the egg yolk. Add the Parmesan cheese and Romano cheese and mix well. Adjust the seasonings to taste.

STUFFED ZUCCHINI WITH BÉCHAMEL SAUCE
SERVES 6

6 (8-inch) zucchini, stem ends trimmed
1 cup minced onion
2 tablespoons unsalted butter
1 cup Béchamel Sauce (page 149)
1/4 cup fine bread crumbs
2 tablespoons freshly grated Parmesan cheese
Salt and pepper to taste
Freshly grated Parmesan cheese
2 tablespoons melted butter
Chopped fresh parsley
Paprika
Lemon wedges for garnish

Slice off the top third of the zucchini lengthwise. Cook the bottoms and top slices in a saucepan of boiling salted water for 10 minutes. Drain, rinse with cold water and drain again. Scoop the pulp carefully onto a cutting board, leaving 1/4-inch shells. Chop the pulp finely and squeeze out as much liquid as possible. Invert the bottom shells onto paper towels to drain and discard the top shells.

Sauté the onion in 2 tablespoons butter in a large skillet until tender but not brown. Stir in the finely chopped zucchini and simmer for 5 minutes. Remove from the heat. Add the Béchamel Sauce, bread crumbs and 2 tablespoons cheese. Season with salt and pepper and mix well. Dry the inside of the zucchini shells with paper towels and spoon the stuffing into the shells. Arrange the stuffed shells in a lightly buttered baking dish. Sprinkle with cheese and drizzle with 2 tablespoons melted butter. Bake in a preheated 450-degree oven for 10 to 15 minutes or until heated through and golden brown.

Remove the stuffed zucchini to a serving platter and sprinkle with chopped parsley and paprika and garnish with lemon wedges.

BÉCHAMEL SAUCE

MAKES ABOUT 2 CUPS

1 tablespoon minced onion
3 tablespoons unsalted butter
1/4 cup all-purpose flour
1 3/4 cups milk, scalded
1/4 cup heavy cream, scalded
1/4 teaspoon salt
White pepper to taste

Sauté the onion in the butter in a saucepan until tender. Stir in the flour. Cook the roux over low heat for 3 minutes, stirring constantly. Remove from the heat and add the hot milk and cream. Whisk until the mixture is thick. Stir in the salt and season with white pepper and return to the heat. Simmer for 10 minutes, stirring occasionally. Strain through a fine sieve into a bowl. Cover the sauce with a buttered round sheet of waxed paper, pressing the waxed paper lightly onto the sauce.

COFFEE-KISSED BAKED BANANAS

SERVES 4

4 firm ripe bananas
1/4 cup (1/2 stick) butter, melted
1/2 teaspoon grated lemon zest
1 tablespoon fresh lemon juice
1/4 cup packed dark brown sugar
1/4 cup coffee liqueur
Vanilla ice cream (optional)

Slice the bananas in half lengthwise and then crosswise. Arrange in an 11×17-inch baking dish. Mix the melted butter, lemon zest and lemon juice in a bowl and drizzle over the bananas. Sprinkle with the brown sugar and drizzle with the coffee liqueur. Bake in a preheated 350-degree oven for 15 minutes. Serve with vanilla ice cream.

PINEAPPLE CASSEROLE
SERVES 6 TO 8

1 (20-ounce) can crushed pineapple in juice
2 eggs, beaten
1 cup sugar
1 cup (2 sticks) margarine, melted
5 to 6 slices white bread, torn into pieces
Milk

Combine the pineapple, eggs, sugar, melted margarine and bread in a bowl and mix well. Spoon into a 1 1/2-quart baking dish. Bake in a preheated 350-degree oven for 25 minutes. Pour enough milk over the top to cover evenly. Bake for 20 minutes longer.

BROWN SUGAR BACON
SERVES 16

2 pounds thick-sliced bacon, cut in half
1 1/2 cups packed brown sugar
1 1/2 teaspoons dry mustard

Arrange the bacon slice halves on a rack in a broiler pan. Combine the brown sugar and dry mustard in a bowl and mix well. Sprinkle evenly over the bacon. Bake in a preheated 250-degree oven for 1 hour.

FARMER'S MARKET
The Charlestown Farmers' Market began in September 2001, under the direction of the Lake Charles Downtown Development Authority. Held each Saturday morning at the Old City Hall Building, built in 1911 and now a cultural center, the market highlights Louisiana homegrown produce including grains, fruits, and vegetables. Additionally, baked goods, flowers, live plants, trees, shrubs, homemade arts and crafts, and literary works are available. The market not only provides a great outlet for local farmers to sell their produce, but also increases awareness of downtown businesses and events.

OYSTERS ROCKEFELLER CASSEROLE

SERVES 8 TO 10

2 (10-ounce) packages frozen spinach
1/4 cup (1/2 stick) butter
1 tablespoon all-purpose flour
2 tablespoons minced onion
1/2 cup evaporated milk
2 1/4 teaspoons celery salt
1/2 teaspoon garlic salt
1/2 teaspoon pepper
1 roll garlic cheese, chopped
2 cups oysters, drained
Salt and pepper to taste
Buttered bread crumbs

Cook the spinach in a saucepan of boiling water according to the package directions. Drain well, reserving 1/2 cup liquid. Melt the butter in a saucepan and stir in the flour. Add the onion and sauté until tender. Stir in the evaporated milk and reserved spinach liquid slowly. Add the celery salt, garlic salt and pepper and cook until thickened, stirring frequently. Stir in the drained spinach and cheese. Spoon into a baking dish. Bake in a preheated 350-degree oven for 20 minutes. Spread the oysters over the bottom of a foil-lined baking pan and season with salt and pepper. Bake in a preheated 400-degree oven for 10 minutes or until the edges are just beginning to curl. Remove the oysters to a baking dish and top with the baked spinach mixture. Sprinkle bread crumbs over the top. Bake in a preheated 350-degree oven for 15 minutes or until heated through and the bread crumbs are golden brown.

OYSTER BREAD DRESSING

SERVES 12

1 onion, chopped
1 bunch shallots, chopped
1 green bell pepper, chopped
4 ribs, celery, chopped
3/4 cup (1 1/2 sticks) butter
8 ounces chicken livers, chopped
2 (10-ounce) jars oysters, drained and liquid reserved
Salt and pepper to taste
1 (8-ounce) package herb-seasoned stuffing

Sauté the onion, shallots, bell pepper and celery in the butter in a large skillet. Add the chicken livers and drained oysters. Cook for 10 minutes, breaking up the oysters with a spoon. Season with salt and pepper. Stir in the stuffing and cook for 20 minutes over low heat, stirring occasionally and adding reserved oyster liquid as needed. Spoon into a buttered baking dish. Bake in a preheated 350-degree oven for 20 minutes.

This recipe may be made ahead without the oysters and chilled. Stir in the oysters and adjust the baking time.

HEARTY CORN BREAD DRESSING
SERVES 12

1 (6-ounce) package corn bread mix,
prepared according to package directions
1 pound lean ground beef
1 bell pepper, chopped
1 onion, chopped
3 ribs celery, chopped
1/2 cup chopped green onions
6 slices dry bread, crumbled
1 teaspoon Italian seasoning
1 (14-ounce) can beef bouillon or broth
1 teaspoon salt
1/2 teaspoon pepper

Let the baked corn bread stand at room temperature for 1 day. Crumble the corn bread into a bowl. Brown the ground beef in a large saucepan, stirring until crumbly; drain. Add the bell pepper, onion, celery and green onions to the saucepan and sauté until the vegetables are tender. Add the crumbled corn bread, dry bread, Italian seasoning, beef bouillon, salt and pepper and mix well. Simmer for 10 minutes and serve.

This dressing freezes well. Thaw before baking and bake in a preheated 350-degree oven for 30 minutes.

Make ahead

Mirepoix
a mixture of diced carrots, onions, celery,
and herbs sautéed in butter

GRITS ON FIRE

SERVES 8

6 cups water
2 cups grits
1/2 cup milk
1/2 cup (1 stick) butter
2 rolls jalapeño cheese
4 eggs, beaten
Salt and pepper to taste
Grated Parmesan cheese to taste
Paprika

Bring the water to a boil in a saucepan and stir in the grits gradually. Cook until the grits are thick and creamy, stirring constantly. Remove from the heat and stir in the milk, butter and jalapeño cheese. Stir in the eggs gradually and season with salt and pepper. Pour into a buttered baking dish and sprinkle with Parmesan cheese and paprika. Bake in a preheated 300-degree oven for 30 minutes. Serve with barbecued chicken.

Grits are small broken grains of corn. They were first produced by Native Americans centuries ago. They are boiled and eaten hot with butter, especially at breakfast in the southern United States. Grits can also be served with cheese, onion, and garlic and are great with shrimp and sausage.

GOAT CHEESE GRITS

SERVES 4

1 cup quick-cooking grits or
stone ground grits
1 tablespoon butter
4 ounces goat cheese
3 tablespoons half-and-half or milk
2 teaspoons chopped fresh parsley
1/4 teaspoon dried basil
1/4 teaspoon coarsely ground black pepper
Salt to taste

Cook the grits until creamy, using the package directions. Add the butter, goat cheese, half-and-half, parsley, basil, pepper and salt and mix well. Cook until the cheese is melted and the mixture is heated through, stirring frequently.

THREE-CHEESE MACARONI WITH CHEDDAR SAUCE

SERVES 8 TO 10

16 ounces macaroni, cooked al dente and drained
3 cups (12 ounces) shredded sharp Cheddar cheese
1 cup (4 ounces) shredded Monterey Jack cheese
1 cup (4 ounces) shredded Colby cheese
4 eggs, beaten
1/2 cup sour cream
1/2 cup (1 stick) butter, melted
1/2 teaspoon salt
2 cups milk
1/4 cup (1/2 stick) butter
1/4 cup all-purpose flour
2 cups milk
Salt and cayenne pepper to taste
1 1/2 cups (6 ounces) shredded Cheddar cheese
4 ounces Velveeta cheese, cubed

Combine the hot macaroni, 3 cups Cheddar cheese, the Monterey Jack cheese and Colby cheese in a large bowl and mix well. Combine the eggs, sour cream, 1/2 cup melted butter, 1/2 teaspoon salt and 2 cups milk in a bowl and mix well. Add to the macaroni and mix well. Spoon into a buttered 9×13-inch baking dish. Bake in a preheated 350-degree oven for 35 to 45 minutes. Melt 1/4 cup butter in a saucepan. Add the flour and cook for 1 minute, stirring constantly. Stir in 2 cups milk and season with salt and cayenne pepper. Cook until thickened, stirring constantly. Add 1 1/2 cups Cheddar cheese and Velveeta cheese and cook until the cheese is melted, stirring constantly. Serve the baked macaroni and cheese topped with the cheese sauce.

BANGKOK CRAB FRIED RICE

SERVES 4 TO 6

1 1/2 to 1 2/3 cups rice
1/4 cup vegetable oil
2 garlic cloves, chopped
4 ounces crab meat, shredded
1 egg
2 teaspoons fish sauce

2 tablespoons light soy sauce
1 teaspoon white pepper
2 tablespoons chopped
   green onions
2 tablespoons chopped
   fresh cilantro

Cook the rice according to the package directions and chill overnight. Heat the oil in a hot wok. Add the garlic and crab meat and cook briefly, stirring constantly. Add the cooked rice and egg and cook briefly, stirring constantly. Stir in the fish sauce, soy sauce and pepper. Cook for 3 minutes over high heat, stirring constantly. Sprinkle with the green onions and coriander and serve.

RICE WITH AN ATTITUDE

SERVES 6

3/4 cup chopped onion
6 tablespoons butter
1 1/4 cups chicken stock
3/4 cup orange juice
1 cup water
3/4 teaspoon Creole seasoning
1 teaspoon salt

1 teaspoon white pepper
1 teaspoon Worcestershire sauce
1 1/2 cups rice
1/2 cup pitted black olives, chopped
1/2 cup pecans, chopped
2 tablespoons chopped
   fresh parsley

Sauté the onion in the butter in a saucepan until tender. Stir in the stock, orange juice, water, Creole seasoning, salt, pepper and Worcestershire sauce and bring to a boil. Stir in the rice and olives. Bring to a boil and reduce the heat. Cook, covered, for 10 minutes. Stir in the pecans and parsley. Cook, covered, for 10 minutes.

Substitute chicken broth when cooking pasta, rice or grits to give extra flavor...or for extra zip, add Zatarain's crab boil to your water.

411 SAUCE

MAKES ABOUT 1/3 CUP

1/4 cup (1/2 stick) butter
1 tablespoon Worcestershire sauce
1 tablespoon fresh lemon juice

Mix the butter, Worcestershire sauce and lemon juice in a saucepan. Cook over low heat until the butter is melted, stirring constantly. Remove from the heat and serve immediately over steak, fish or chicken.

WHITE BARBECUE CHICKEN SAUCE

MAKES ABOUT 5 CUPS

3 large onions, chopped
2 cups (4 sticks) margarine
1/2 cup water
1/4 cup Worcestershire sauce
Juice of 2 lemons
1 tablespoon Tabasco sauce
1 1/2 tablespoons sugar

Sauté the onions in the margarine in a saucepan until translucent. Stir in the water, Worcestershire sauce, lemon juice, Tabasco sauce and sugar. Cook over low heat for 30 to 40 minutes, stirring occasionally. Brush over chicken as it grills. Heat the remaining sauce to boiling and boil for 2 minutes. Pour over the cooked chicken.

OLD WORLD SWEET-AND-SOUR SAUCE

MAKES 1 CUP

1/3 cup vinegar
1/3 cup pineapple juice
1/3 cup sugar
1 teaspoon salt, or to taste
1/4 teaspoon pepper, or to taste
1/2 teaspoon ketchup
1 teaspoon Worcestershire sauce
1 garlic clove, crushed
2 slices fresh ginger, crushed
1 teaspoon minced shallots
1 teaspoon soy sauce

Combine the vinegar, pineapple juice and sugar in a saucepan and bring to a boil, stirring constantly. Stir in the salt, pepper, ketchup, Worcestershire sauce, garlic, ginger, shallots and soy sauce. Cook to the desired consistency, stirring constantly. Strain the sauce into a container.

A thin consistency is generally preferred for table use. A thick consistency is generally preferred for use with spareribs, duck or fish.

For delicious spareribs, simmer deep-fried spareribs in the sauce for 2 hours.

Coulis
A thick sauce or purée

SAFFRON BEURRE BLANC

MAKES ABOUT ¹/₂ CUP

2 Key limes
1 lemon
White wine vinegar
2 garlic cloves, pressed
¹/₄ cup (¹/₂ stick) unsalted butter, cut into 8 pieces
¹/₄ teaspoon chopped saffron threads

Juice the Key limes and lemon and pour into a glass measuring cup. Add an equal amount of vinegar to the juice. Pour the mixture into a heavy saucepan. Cook over medium-high heat until reduced to ¹/₄ cup. Reduce the heat to medium. Cook until reduced to 3 tablespoons. Stir in the garlic and remove from the heat. Add two pieces of butter and whisk until the butter is melted. Whisk in the remaining butter, one piece at a time, whisking until the butter is melted before adding more. Return the saucepan to the off but still warm burner. Spoon some of the sauce onto serving plates and sprinkle each with a few saffron threads. Top with cooked fish fillets, the remaining sauce and sprinkle with the remaining saffron threads.

LEMON BUTTER CAPER SAUCE

MAKES ABOUT ¹/₂ CUP

¹/₄ cup chardonnay
2 tablespoons fresh lemon juice
¹/₂ cup (1 stick) unsalted butter
3 tablespoons extra-virgin olive oil
2 garlic cloves, pressed
1 pinch saffron threads, cut into ¹/₄-inch pieces (optional)
1 teaspoon sea salt, or to taste
¹/₄ teaspoon white pepper
2 tablespoons drained capers

Cook the chardonnay and lemon juice in a saucepan over medium heat until reduced by two-thirds. Add the butter, olive oil and garlic and cook until creamy, whisking constantly. Add the saffron, salt and pepper and cook to the desired consistency, whisking constantly. Stir in the capers and serve over sautéed fish fillets.

CRAWFISH

Dating back to Native Americans and early European settlers, crawfish have always been an inherent part of Louisiana culture. Abundant in the swamps and marshes across South Louisiana, crawfish were a favorite food of early inhabitants. Centuries later, the crawfish season in Louisiana is a much-anticipated rite of spring, with crawfish boils and backyard parties almost every weekend. Louisiana has more than thirty different crawfish species and the farming of this delicacy has developed into the largest freshwater crustacean aquaculture industry in the United States. Louisiana leads the nation by producing more than 90 percent of the domestic crop.

In Cajun country, the most common crop rotation when raising crawfish is the rice-crawfish-rice rotation. After farmers plant and harvest their rice, they fertilize and flood the remaining stems as food for crawfish. Traps are placed in the fields, which enables the farmers to yield thousands of pounds of crawfish each season.

Saffron Butter Cream Sauce

Serves 4

1/2 cup (1 stick) butter
1/2 cup extra-virgin olive oil
1 teaspoon minced fresh thyme
1 teaspoon minced fresh oregano
1 tablespoon minced fresh sweet basil
6 garlic cloves, minced
1/2 yellow onion, minced
2 tablespoons shrimp stock
Juice of 1 lemon
Juice of 1/2 lime
1 pinch of saffron threads, ground with a mortar and pestle
2 portobello mushrooms, cut into 1-inch cubes
1 teaspoon salt
1 teaspoon freshly ground pepper
1 1/2 cups fat-free half-and-half
1 tablespoon cornstarch
2 tablespoons cold water
Hot cooked linguini
Freshly grated Parmigiano-Reggiano cheese

Melt the butter in a saucepan and stir in the olive oil. Bring to a simmer and stir in the thyme, oregano, basil, garlic and onion. Simmer until the onion is light brown, stirring frequently. Stir in the stock, lemon juice, lime juice and saffron. Simmer until the color is uniform, stirring constantly. Add the mushrooms, salt and pepper and sauté until the mushrooms are tender and most of the mushroom liquid has evaporated. Stir in the half-and-half and simmer for 5 minutes. Dissolve the cornstarch in the water in a bowl and stir into the sauce. Cook over medium heat until thickened, stirring constantly. Serve over hot linguini and top with cheese.

CLASSIC BÉARNAISE SAUCE
SERVES 4

1 cup (2 sticks) unsalted butter, cut into tablespoons
1 cup Pouilly Fuisse white wine or chardonnay
1 tablespoon tarragon vinegar
1 tablespoon minced shallots
1 sprig flat-leaf parsley, coarsely chopped
2 tablespoons minced tarragon leaves
2 (8-inch) tender tarragon stalks, coarsely chopped
$1/2$ teaspoon dried chervil
$1/2$ teaspoon sea salt
$1/8$ teaspoon freshly ground black pepper
3 egg yolks, lightly beaten
$1/8$ teaspoon cayenne pepper
1 teaspoon minced tarragon leaves
$1/2$ teaspoon dried chervil

Melt the butter in a heavy saucepan. Reduce the heat to very low and keep warm. Combine the wine, vinegar, shallots, parsley, 2 tablespoons tarragon leaves, the tarragon stalks, $1/2$ teaspoon chervil, the salt and black pepper in a heavy saucepan. Cook over high heat until the mixture is reduced by two-thirds, stirring occasionally.

Remove the saucepan to 1 inch of cold water in a sink for 30 seconds to cool slightly. Return the saucepan to very low heat. Whisk in one-third of the egg yolks and then whisk in one-third of the melted butter. Repeat two more times to use the remaining egg yolks and butter. Cook until the sauce is the consistency of heavy cream, whisking constantly.

Strain the sauce through a fine sieve into the saucepan that held the butter. Add the cayenne pepper, 1 teaspoon tarragon and $1/2$ teaspoon chervil. Cook over very low heat until thickened, whisking constantly. Serve immediately over sautéed fish fillets.

CALCASIEU SEASONING MIX

MAKES 2 1/2 CUPS

1/3 cup salt
1/4 cup garlic powder
1/4 cup black pepper
1/4 cup white pepper
2 tablespoons cayenne pepper
2 tablespoons ground thyme
1 tablespoon oregano
1/3 cup paprika
2 tablespoons plus 2 teaspoons onion powder
2 tablespoons plus 2 teaspoons dried sweet basil
1/3 teaspoon dried rosemary
1/4 teaspoon cumin
1/4 teaspoon fennel seeds,
ground with a mortar and pestle

Process the salt, garlic powder, black pepper, white pepper, cayenne pepper, thyme, oregano, paprika, onion powder, basil, rosemary, cumin and fennel seeds in a food processor to mix well. Store in a jar with a tight-fitting lid.

Lagniappe
A little something extra
and unexpected

THE SWEET LIFE
Desserts

Just as family and friends add sweetness to our lives, so too

do art and music. We live for the sweet life in Southwest Louisiana,

and fortunately, we have plenty of it to go around!

Our region is home to some of the oldest arts organizations in the state.

We boast a community theater that is nearly eighty years old. We're very

proud to be the birthplace of many Cajun and zydeco musicians, and the

cradle of a brand of music all our own; it's called swamp pop, and it's a

down-home blend of boogie and blues that sets the soul and feet on fire.

The desserts in this section will add a sweet finish to your meal.

This chapter of the book brings you to what some would

say is the best part. So choose the dessert that will give your meal

its grand finale, and always remember to . . .

Laissez les bon temps roulez!

Desserts

Amaretto Bread Pudding 167 · White Chocolate Blueberry Bread Pudding 168

Amaretto Cheesecake 169 · Napa Valley Cheesecake 170 · Pots de Crème 171 · Pumpkin Delight 172

Pistachio Parfait 173 · Praline Torte 173 · Microwave Pralines 173 · Strawberry Cheesecake Trifle 174

Caramel Apple Crunch 175 · Apple Dew Delight 176 · Country Blackberry Cobbler 177

Drunken Strawberries 177 · Crepes Suzette 178 · Blueberry Tart 179 · Buttermilk Pie 180

Lemon Tequila Pie 181 · Easy Peanut Butter Pie 181 · "Chocolate Lovers" Chocolate Pie 182

Almond Cake with Raspberry Sauce 183 · Turtle Cake 184 · Grandmother's Chocolate Cake 185

Chocolate Kahlúa Cake 186 · Dreamy Coconut Cake 187 · Key Lime Cake 188

Buttermilk Fig Cake 189 · Tropical Paradise Cake 192 · Mardi Gras King Cake 193

Pistachio Nut Swirl Cake 194 · Favorite Pound Cake 194 · Walnut Rum Spice Cake 195

Chocolate Crinkles 196 · Chocolate Oatmeal Cookies 196 · Button Cookies 197

Graham Cracker Cookies 197 · Brownie Mallow Bars 198 · Ooey-Gooey Caramel Brownies 198

Crème de Menthe Bars 199 · Praline Pecan Bites 200 · Gentleman's Bourbon Balls 201

Chocolate Kisses 201 · Almond Butter Toffee 202 · Toasted Pecan Clusters 203

Zapped Peanut Brittle 203 · Cowboy Candy 204 · Chocolate Toffee Crunch 205

Peppermint Bark 206 · Chocolate Party Mix 206

AMARETTO BREAD PUDDING

SERVES 10 TO 12

4 cups half-and-half
1 loaf French bread, torn into 1-inch pieces
3 eggs
1 1/2 cups granulated sugar
2 to 3 tablespoons almond extract
1 cup sliced almonds
1/2 cup golden raisins (optional)
2 tablespoons unsalted butter, softened
1/2 cup (1 stick) unsalted butter, softened
1 cup confectioners' sugar
1 egg, beaten
1/4 to 1/3 cup amaretto or almond-flavored liqueur

Pour the half-and-half evenly over the bread in a large bowl. Let stand for 1 hour. Beat 3 eggs lightly in a bowl. Add the granulated sugar and almond extract and mix well. Pour over the bread mixture and mix well. Fold in the almonds and raisins. Grease a baking dish with 2 tablespoons butter. Spread the bread mixture into the prepared baking dish. Bake in a preheated 325-degree oven for 50 to 60 minutes or until golden brown. Combine 1/2 cup butter and confectioners' sugar in the top of a double boiler over simmering water. Cook until the mixture is very hot, stirring constantly. Remove the top of the double boiler from the water and slowly whisk in 1 beaten egg. Let cool slightly and stir in the amaretto. Spoon the sauce evenly over the baked pudding. Broil 3 to 4 inches from the heat source until the sauce is bubbly. Remove to a wire rack and let cool.

GALLERY PROMENADE

The arts are alive in Southwest Louisiana! And when we celebrate the visual arts we promenade. Home to world-renowned artists and musicians in many genres, Southwest Louisiana loves nothing more than showing off our talented artisans. Known as Gallery Promenade, many Southwest Louisiana galleries and museums open to celebrate and support the arts once a year. When we promenade, we spend an entire evening, and often the next day, attending exhibitions, sampling local delicacies, and enjoying the company of all those who love the arts. Whether you're browsing or buying, the Gallery Promenade offers something creative and unique for everyone.

WHITE CHOCOLATE BLUEBERRY BREAD PUDDING

SERVES 24

12 to 18 miniature croissants
12 eggs
2 cups sugar
1 cup sweetened condensed milk
$1/4$ cup vanilla extract
4 cups fresh blueberries
$1/2$ cup pecans
1 cup (2 sticks) butter
$5^1/3$ cups white chocolate chips
6 tablespoons whiskey

Tear the croissants into pieces and spread over the bottom of a greased 9×13-inch baking dish. Combine the eggs, sugar, sweetened condensed milk and vanilla in a bowl and mix well. Pour evenly over the croissants. Sprinkle the blueberries and pecans over the top. Bake in a preheated 350-degree oven for 50 minutes. Remove to a wire rack. Combine the butter and white chocolate chips in the top of a double boiler over simmering water. Cook until the mixture is melted and smooth, whisking constantly. Stir in the whiskey just before serving. Serve the bread pudding with the sauce over the top or on the side.

Prix Fixe

a "fixed" or preset price for a restaurant meal.
It is often a feature of a special occasion event.

AMARETTO CHEESECAKE

SERVES 10 TO 12

1 to 1 1/2 cups graham cracker crumbs or
chocolate cookie crumbs
1/2 cup confectioners' sugar
3/4 cup (1 1/2 sticks) butter, melted
24 ounces cream cheese, softened
3 eggs
1 (14-ounce) can sweetened
condensed milk
6 tablespoons amaretto, or 2 to 3 teaspoons
almond extract

Combine the graham cracker crumbs, confectioners' sugar and melted butter in a bowl and mix well. Press over the bottom and up the side of a 9-inch springform pan.

Beat the cream cheese in a mixing bowl until smooth. Add the eggs, one at a time, beating well after each addition. Beat in the sweetened condensed milk and amaretto. Scrape the side of the bowl and beat for 1 to 2 minutes. Pour into the prepared crust and tap the pan to remove any air bubbles. Place the springform pan in a larger baking pan. Add enough hot water to the larger pan to come halfway up the sides of the springform pan. Bake in a preheated 300- to 325-degree oven for 70 to 80 minutes or until the center of the cheesecake is firm when touched. Remove the springform pan to a wire rack to cool completely. Chill, covered, until cold. Loosen from the side of the pan with a sharp knife and remove the side.

To make a water bath, place the item to be cooked in a shallow pan of water. The water heats and cooks the item gently. The baking dish containing the water and the item to be cooked are generally porcelain or ceramic.

NAPA VALLEY CHEESECAKE

SERVES 12

1 (2-layer) package yellow cake mix
1/2 cup (1 stick) butter, melted
1 egg
1 tablespoon milk
1/2 cup finely chopped pecans
1 (16-ounce) package confectioners' sugar
3 eggs
8 ounces cream cheese, softened
1 1/2 teaspoons vanilla extract

Combine the cake mix, melted butter, 1 egg, the milk and pecans in a bowl and mix well. Press over the bottom of a nonstick 10×13-inch or 10×15-inch baking pan. Beat the confectioners' sugar, 3 eggs, cream cheese and vanilla in a mixing bowl. Pour over the prepared crust. Bake in a 350-degree oven for 45 to 60 minutes or until the top is light brown. Remove to a wire rack to cool. Cut into squares and serve with strawberries and ice cream, if desired.

ARTS & HUMANITIES CENTER

Central School Arts and Humanities Center is an historic school that served generations of Lake Charles students and is now playing a new role for them, their children, and their grandchildren.

Championed by historic preservationists and arts advocates in the early 1990s, the restoration of the Central School in Lake Charles and its transformation into the Central School Arts and Humanities Center is having a tremendous impact on the community. With the future of the 1912 structure in doubt after fire code violations had forced its closure, the community's desire to save it was expressed in a number of ways, including a willingness to approve a tax levy to finance its renovation. What is truly unique about the Lake Charles experience was that citizens were willing to freely tax themselves to save a structure that not only was historic in its architecture, but also held so many memories for Lake Charles' families. Today, the adaptive reuse of Central School as a thriving arts and humanities center is also a catalyst in the downtown and historic district development.

POTS DE CRÈME

SERVES 5

1 cup (6 ounces) semisweet chocolate chips
1 egg
2 tablespoons granulated sugar
1 teaspoon vanilla extract
Pinch of salt
3/4 cup milk
Confectioners' sugar

Combine the chocolate chips, egg, granulated sugar, vanilla and salt in a blender container. Heat the milk in a saucepan just to boiling and add to the blender container. Process at low speed for 1 minute. Pour into five pots de crème cups or ramekins. Chill for several hours or until cold. Dust with confectioners' sugar before serving.

   If you are concerned about using raw eggs, use eggs pasteurized in their shells, which are sold at some specialty food stores, or use an equivalent amount of pasteurized egg substitute.

Pots de Crème

This custard received its name from the individual lidded porcelain pots in which it is traditionally baked.

PUMPKIN DELIGHT

SERVES 15

1 3/4 cups graham cracker crumbs
1/4 cup sugar
1/2 cup (1 stick) butter or
margarine, melted
8 ounces cream cheese, softened
2 eggs, beaten
3/4 cup sugar
2 (3-ounce) packages vanilla instant
pudding mix
3/4 cup milk
2 cups mashed cooked pumpkin or
canned pumpkin
Dash of ground cinnamon
1 (8-ounce) container frozen whipped
topping, thawed

Combine the graham cracker crumbs, 1/4 cup sugar and the melted butter in a bowl and mix well. Press over the bottom of a 9×13-inch baking dish. Beat the cream cheese, eggs and 3/4 cup sugar in a mixing bowl until light and fluffy. Spread over the prepared crust. Bake in a preheated 350-degree oven for 20 minutes. Remove to a wire rack and let cool completely.

Beat the pudding mix and milk in a mixing bowl at medium speed for 2 minutes. Add the pumpkin and cinnamon and mix well. Stir in 1 cup of the whipped topping. Spread over the cooled baked layer. Spread the remaining whipped topping over the pumpkin layer. Chill until ready to serve.

Bienvenue en Louisiane

Welcome to Louisiana. These signs are placed at the Louisiana borders to greet highway drivers to our wonderful state.

PISTACHIO PARFAIT

SERVES 8

1 (20-ounce) can crushed pineapple
8 ounces cream cheese, softened
1 (4-ounce) package pistachio instant pudding mix
1 cup chopped pecans
8 ounces whipped topping
Whipped topping for garnish
Chopped pecans for garnish
Chopped maraschino cherries for garnish

Drain the pineapple, reserving the juice. Beat the cream cheese in a mixing bowl until smooth and creamy. Add the pudding mix and beat until blended. Add the reserved pineapple juice and mix well. Beat in the pineapple and 1 cup pecans until combined. Fold in 8 ounces whipped topping.

Spoon the cream cheese mixture into a serving bowl and chill, covered, for up to 5 days. Garnish with whipped topping, chopped pecans and/or chopped maraschino cherries.

PRALINE TORTE

SERVES 10 TO 12

16 ounces mascarpone cheese
6 firm pralines, crumbled (2 to 3 ounces)
1 jar seedless raspberry jam
Gingersnaps or graham crackers

Line a bowl with plastic wrap. Alternate layers of the cheese and crumbled pralines in the prepared bowl. Chill, covered, for 1 hour. Unmold the torte onto a serving plate and remove the plastic wrap. Heat the jam in the microwave or in a saucepan. Pour over the torte and serve with gingersnaps.

HOLLYWOOD SOUTH

Louisiana—Hollywood South? Due to the Legislator's creation of generous tax credits, Louisiana has gone Hollywood! Today, you may find yourself bumping into Jude Law, Denzel Washington, Sean Penn, Brad Pitt, or Hillary Swank, as they work on movies and experience Louisiana's unique and authentic culture while not on set. Movies filmed in Louisiana include Runaway Jury, The Dukes of Hazzard, Ray, Elvis, Monster's Ball, All the King's Men, *and many more.*

To prepare Microwave Pralines, combine 1 cup granulated sugar, 1 cup packed brown sugar, 1 (5-ounce) can evaporated milk, 1 teaspoon vanilla extract and 1 1/4 cups pecans in a microwave-safe bowl. Microwave for 10 minutes, stirring once halfway through the cooking process. Beat until blended. Drop by spoonfuls onto waxed paper and let stand until set.

STRAWBERRY CHEESECAKE TRIFLE

SERVES 24

ZYDECO

Zydeco (pronounced ZY-duh-coe) is the exuberant dance music of Southwest Louisiana's black Creoles. Stylistically, it is a rich hybrid, with a core of Afro-Caribbean rhythms and folk roots, blues, and Cajun music (zydeco's white counterpart), along with a wealth of other elements. These vary widely from band to band and may include rock, country, R&B, reggae, rap, and hip-hop. Traditionally, zydeco is sung in French, and the lyrics are often improvised. It is absolutely not intended for passive listening, as it definitely stimulates dancing.

Zydeco's dominant instrument is the accordion, which is sometimes referred to as a squeezebox. It is played by compression and expansion of a bellow which causes air to flow across reeds. A keyboard with buttons or piano-style keys controls which reed receives the airflow and, in turn, the tone.

Frottoir, or rub board, is the signature musical instrument in zydeco music. It is fashioned from a vest and worn over the shoulders in front of the body. Spoons or paint can openers are used to rub against the ridges of the metal board to resonate a unique sound.

16 ounces cream cheese, softened
2 cups confectioners' sugar
1 cup sour cream
1/2 teaspoon vanilla extract
1/4 teaspoon almond extract
1 cup heavy whipping cream
1 teaspoon vanilla extract
1 tablespoon granulated sugar
1 baked angel food cake, torn into bite-size pieces
8 cups fresh strawberries, thinly sliced
3 tablespoons granulated sugar
3 tablespoons almond-flavored liqueur, or
almond extract to taste

Beat the cream cheese and confectioners' sugar in a large bowl until light and fluffy. Add the sour cream, 1/2 teaspoon vanilla and 1/4 teaspoon almond extract and mix well. Whip the cream, 1 teaspoon vanilla and 1 tablespoon granulated sugar in a bowl until stiff. Fold into the cream cheese mixture. Fold in the cake pieces. Combine the strawberries, 3 tablespoons granulated sugar and liqueur in a bowl and mix well. Alternate layers of the strawberries and the cake mixture in a trifle bowl or large glass bowl, beginning and ending with the strawberries. Chill, covered, until cold. Serve the same day.

Try adding a layer or two of blueberries for a wonderful 4th of July dessert.

CARAMEL APPLE CRUNCH

SERVES 16

16 ounces cream cheese, softened
1 1/4 cups confectioners' sugar
2 large red apples
2 large green apples
Fruit Fresh (fruit color protector)
Lemon juice
1 cup caramel dip (found in the produce section)
3 chocolate-covered toffee bars, crushed

Beat the cream cheese and confectioners' sugar in a mixing bowl until light and fluffy. Chill for at least 15 minutes. Core and slice the red and green apples and place in a bowl. Sprinkle with Fruit Fresh and lemon juice and add cold water to cover the apples. Spread the cream cheese mixture into a 9-inch layer on a 12- to 16-inch serving plate. Spread the caramel sauce over the cream cheese layer and top with the crushed candy. Drain the apple slices and arrange alternating colors around the edge of the plate.

Make ahead

Cane Syrup a thick and intensely sweet syrup made from sugar cane. It's a must on hot southern biscuits

APPLE DEW DELIGHT

SERVES 16

2 (8-count) cans refrigerator crescent rolls
2 large Granny Smith apples, peeled, cored and
cut into eighths
1 cup (2 sticks) margarine, melted
1 1/2 cups sugar
1 1/2 teaspoons cinnamon
1 (12-ounce) can Mountain Dew soda

Separate each can of crescent rolls into eight pieces on a work surface. Roll one apple slice in each crescent dough piece, starting at the wide end. Arrange the apple rolls in a 9×13-inch baking dish. Combine the melted margarine, sugar and cinnamon in a bowl and mix well. Pour the margarine mixture evenly over the apple rolls. Pour the soda around the edges of the apple rolls but not over the top. Bake in a preheated 350-degree oven for 45 minutes.

Demitasse

A tiny half-cup used to serve strong Louisiana coffee

COUNTRY BLACKBERRY COBBLER

SERVES 6 TO 8

2 heaping cups blackberries
2 cups sugar
1 cup all-purpose flour
1 cup sugar
2 teaspoons baking powder
1/2 teaspoon salt
3/4 cup (1 1/2 sticks) butter, softened
3/4 cup milk

Combine the blackberries and 2 cups sugar in a bowl and mix gently. Let stand for 2 hours. Mix the flour, 1 cup sugar, the baking powder and salt in a bowl. Cut in the butter with a pastry blender or fork until crumbly. Add the milk and stir just until moistened. Spread into a baking dish. Spoon the blackberries evenly over the top; do not stir. Bake, covered, in a preheated 350 degree oven for 1 hour. Serve with cream or ice cream.

Peaches, blueberries or your favorite sweet fruit may be substituted for the blackberries.

DRUNKEN STRAWBERRIES

SERVES 8

1 cup (or less) cabernet sauvignon or bordeaux
2 to 3 tablespoons sugar
2 pounds fresh strawberries, sliced
1 package brownie mix
French vanilla, Mexican vanilla or
vanilla bean ice cream

Mix the wine and sugar in a bowl until the sugar dissolves. Add the strawberries and mix until coated. Let stand at room temperature for 2 hours or longer, stirring occasionally.

Prepare the brownies using the package directions. Cut the warm brownies into squares. Arrange the brownie squares on individual dessert plates and top each with a scoop of ice cream and some of the strawberry mixture. Serve immediately.

JURÉ

Juré is an African-American vocal tradition sung in French Creole, accompanied only by hand clapping and foot stomping. Juré is one of several root sources for zydeco music. Although some juré songs are religious, others are secular and spontaneously improvised. Sadly, today Juré singing has all but disappeared.

CREPES SUZETTE

SERVES 12

Kirsch, is a clear brandy made
from double distillation of the
fermented juice of small black
cherries. Unlike cherry liqueurs,
Kirsch is not sweet.

To get the highest beaten egg
whites, whip egg whites that are
at room temperature, not cold.
An egg's protein is more elastic
and will create more tiny air
bubbles when at room temperature.
Also, the colder the egg, the
longer the beating time will be.
If it is humid or raining outside,
sometimes you won't get the
proper volume no matter what
you do.

CREPES

2 cups all-purpose flour
2 tablespoons granulated sugar
1/2 teaspoon salt
4 eggs
4 egg yolks
3 cups milk
1/2 cup whipping cream
1/4 cup (1/2 stick) unsalted butter, melted
2 tablespoons cognac
1/2 cup (1 stick) unsalted butter, softened
1 (16-ounce) package confectioners' sugar
1 teaspoon vanilla extract
Grated zest of 1 orange
2 to 4 tablespoons cognac

CREPE SAUCE

1 cup cognac
1 cup Grand Marnier
1/2 cup orange curaçao
1/2 cup Triple Sec
1/4 cup kirsch
1/4 cup granulated sugar
1 tablespoon grated orange zest
Additional grated orange zest

CREPES

Mix the flour, granulated sugar and salt in a bowl. Beat the eggs and egg yolks in a bowl and whisk in the milk and cream. Whisk the egg mixture gradually into the dry ingredients and whisk until smooth. Stir in 1/4 cup melted butter and 2 tablespoons cognac. Let stand for 2 hours. Pour 3 tablespoons batter into a hot heavy nonstick skillet and swirl the pan to coat the bottom with batter. Cook for 1 minute per side and remove to a plate. Repeat to use the remaining batter and add the cooked crepes to the plate. Beat 1/2 cup butter and confectioners' sugar in a bowl until light and fluffy. Add the vanilla, orange zest and half the cognac and mix well. Stir in enough remaining cognac to make a smooth paste. Chill for 2 hours. Lay the crepes on a work surface. Spread the cream cheese mixture over the crepes and fold in half and in half again. Arrange the filled crepes in a copper serving skillet and chill.

CREPE SAUCE

Combine the cognac, Grand Marnier, orange curaçao, Triple Sec, kirsch, sugar and 1 tablespoon orange zest in a bowl and mix well. Pour over the crepes in the serving skillet. Cook over low heat until warm. Ignite the sauce with a long match and carefully spoon the flaming sauce over the crepes with a long-handled spoon. Remove the crepes to serving plates when the flames die out. Top with the sauce and sprinkle with orange zest.

Blueberry Tart
Serves 8

Tart Pastry
2 cups all-purpose flour
11 tablespoons butter
$^1/_4$ teaspoon salt
Pinch of sugar
5 to 6 tablespoons ice water

Blueberry Filling
$^1/_2$ cup sugar
2 tablespoons cornstarch
Pinch of salt
$^1/_4$ cup water
3 cups fresh or frozen blueberries, thawed
4 cups fresh blueberries

Pastry
Process the flour, butter, salt and sugar in a food processor until the mixture resembles coarse crumbs. Remove to a bowl. Stir in the ice water gradually with a fork. Turn the dough out onto a lightly floured work surface and knead gently two or three times. Shape the dough into a disk and place in a sealable plastic bag. Seal the bag and chill for 1 to 2 hours. Roll out the dough on a floured work surface or waxed paper. Fit into a 10-inch tart pan and trim the edges. Prick the dough with a fork at $^1/_2$-inch intervals. Place a sheet of buttered foil over the dough and fill the foil with pie weights or 1 to 2 cups dried beans. Bake in a preheated 400-degree oven for 10 minutes. Remove the foil with weights and bake for 7 to 10 minutes longer or until golden brown. Remove to a wire rack to cool.

Filling
Mix the sugar, cornstarch and salt in a saucepan. Stir in the water. Add 3 cups blueberries. Bring to a simmer over low heat, stirring occasionally. Simmer for 5 to 8 minutes, stirring occasionally. Remove from the heat and let cool. Pour into the baked crust. Top with 4 cups blueberries.

BUTTERMILK PIE

SERVES 6 TO 8

1 1/2 cups sugar
3 eggs
1/2 cup baking mix
1 cup buttermilk
5 1/3 tablespoons (1/3 cup) unsalted butter
1 teaspoon vanilla extract

Combine the sugar, eggs, baking mix and buttermilk in a bowl and mix well. Melt the butter in a 9-inch pie plate in the oven. Pour the melted butter into the buttermilk mixture, leaving a small amount of melted butter to coat the pie plate. Add the vanilla to the buttermilk mixture and mix well. Pour into the pie plate. Bake in a preheated 350-degree oven for 25 to 30 minutes or until a knife inserted in the center comes out clean. Remove to a wire rack to cool.

Garde-Manger

Pie safe or a pantry used to store pies and other food items in an area that was cool and well-ventilated; in other words, it was "safe" to keep the food there

LEMON TEQUILA PIE

SERVES 6 TO 8

24 graham crackers, crushed
1/4 cup packed brown sugar
1/4 cup (1/2 stick) butter, melted
3 eggs, beaten
1 (14-ounce) can sweetened condensed milk
1/2 cup lemon juice
1/4 cup tequila
1 cup sour cream
3 tablespoons granulated sugar

Combine the graham cracker crumbs, brown sugar and melted butter in a bowl and mix well. Press over the bottom and up the side of a 9-inch pie plate. Whisk the eggs and sweetened condensed milk in a saucepan. Whisk in the lemon juice and tequila. Bring just to a boil, stirring constantly. Remove from the heat and let cool for 5 to 10 minutes. Pour into the prepared crust. Mix the sour cream and granulated sugar in a bowl and spread over the lemon filling. Chill for at least 2 hours before serving.

Make ahead

How to make brown sugar: Mix 1 cup granulated sugar with 1/2 cup molasses to yield 1 cup brown sugar.

EASY PEANUT BUTTER PIE

SERVES 16

8 ounces cream cheese, softened
2 cups confectioners' sugar
3/4 to 1 cup peanut butter
20 ounces frozen whipped topping, thawed
2 (9-inch) graham cracker pie shells
Chocolate syrup
Chopped peanuts

Combine the cream cheese and confectioners' sugar in a bowl and mix well. Stir in the peanut butter. Fold in the whipped topping. Spoon into the pie shells. Drizzle with chocolate syrup and sprinkle with chopped peanuts.
   This pie freezes well.

Make ahead

Make sure your whipping cream, bowl, and beater are COLD for best results. Be sure bowls are completely free of grease or oil.

"CHOCOLATE LOVERS" CHOCOLATE PIE
SERVES 15

NUTTY CRUST
1 cup sifted all-purpose flour
1/4 cup packed brown sugar
1/4 cup chopped walnuts or pecans
1/2 cup (1 stick) unsalted butter

CHOCOLATE FILLING
2 cups (12 ounces) semisweet
chocolate chips
1/4 cup granulated sugar
1/4 cup milk

4 egg yolks
1 teaspoon vanilla extract
4 egg whites
1 teaspoon salt
2 cups heavy whipping cream
1/4 cup confectioners' sugar,
  or to taste
2 cups heavy whipping cream
1/4 cup confectioners' sugar,
  or to taste
1 chocolate candy bar, shaved

NUTTY CRUST
Combine the flour, brown sugar and walnuts in a bowl and mix well. Add the
butter and stir until crumbly. Pat the crumb mixture in a 9×13-inch baking dish;
it is not necessary to cover the entire bottom of the dish. Bake in a preheated
400-degree oven for 15 minutes. Remove from the oven and immediately stir
the baked crumb mixture. Press evenly over the bottom and let stand until cool.

CHOCOLATE FILLING
Combine the chocolate chips, granulated sugar and milk in a double boiler
and cook until blended, stirring frequently. Spoon the chocolate mixture into
a mixing bowl and beat lightly with an electric mixer. Add the egg yolks one
at a time, beating well after each addition. Mix in the vanilla. Beat the egg
whites and salt in a mixing bowl until stiff peaks form and fold into the
chocolate mixture.
　　Beat 2 cups whipping cream in a mixing bowl until soft peaks form. Beat in
1/4 cup confectioners' sugar. Fold the whipped cream into the chocolate mixture
and spread over the baked layer. Chill, covered, until set.
　　Beat 2 cups whipping cream in a mixing bowl until soft peaks form. Beat in
1/4 cup confectioners' sugar. Spread the whipped cream over the chilled layers
and sprinkle with the shaved chocolate. Chill, covered, until serving time.

ALMOND CAKE WITH RASPBERRY SAUCE
SERVES 8

ALMOND CAKE
1 (8-ounce) package almond paste
3/4 cup granulated sugar
1/2 cup (1 stick) unsalted
    butter, softened
3 eggs, at room temperature
1 tablespoon amaretto
1/4 teaspoon almond extract
1/4 cup all-purpose flour

1/3 teaspoon baking powder
Confectioners' sugar

RASPBERRY SAUCE
2 cups fresh raspberries, or
    1 (12-ounce) package frozen
    raspberries, thawed
2 tablespoons sugar, or to taste
Amaretto to taste

CAKE
Soften the almond paste in the microwave for a few seconds. Combine the almond paste, granulated sugar and butter in a bowl and mix well. Beat in the eggs, amaretto and almond extract. Add the flour and baking powder and mix just until blended. Pour into a generously buttered and floured 8-inch cake pan. Bake in a preheated 350-degree oven for 35 to 40 minutes or until a wooden pick inserted in the center comes out clean. Cool in the pan for 10 minutes. Remove to a wire rack to cool completely. Place the cake on a serving plate and dust lightly with confectioners' sugar.

SAUCE
Process the raspberries in a blender or food processor unil puréed. Add the sugar and amaretto and process to mix. Press through a fine sieve into a serving bowl and serve with the almond cake.

To make your own almond paste try the following: Make sugar syrup by placing 1 cup water, 5 ounces sugar, and 1/4 cup corn syrup in saucepan. Boil for a few seconds and cool. Place 10 ounces dried blanched almonds in food processor and process to a fine powder. Add 10 ounces powdered sugar. With the food processor running, slowly add the sugar syrup until the mixture forms a paste. Store tightly covered.

When you forget to take the butter out of the refrigerator to soften do not use the microwave or you will have a butter puddle. Instead, to soften butter quickly, unwrap a stick of butter and place it in a resealable plastic bag. Use a rolling pin to beat and flatten the butter, and it will be soft in no time.

TURTLE CAKE
SERVES 12

1 (14-ounce) package caramels
3/4 cup (1 1/2 sticks) butter
1/2 cup evaporated milk
1 (2-layer) package German chocolate cake mix
1 cup (6 ounces) chocolate chips
1 cup pecans, chopped
8 ounces frozen whipped topping, thawed

Combine the caramels, butter and evaporated milk in a microwave-safe dish. Microwave until blended, stirring frequently.

Prepare the cake mix using the package directions. Spread half the batter in a greased and floured 9×13-inch cake pan. Bake in a preheated 350-degree oven for 15 minutes. Remove from the oven and sprinkle with the chocolate chips and pecans. Drizzle with the caramel mixture and spread with the remaining batter.

Bake for 20 minutes longer. Cool in the pan on a wire rack. Spread with the whipped topping and serve immediately. Store leftovers in the refrigerator.

Café au Lait

coffee with scalded milk

GRANDMOTHER'S CHOCOLATE CAKE
SERVES 15

CHOCOLATE CAKE
2 cups all-purpose flour
2 cups sugar
1/4 cup baking cocoa
1/2 cup (1 stick) butter
1 cup water
1/2 cup vegetable oil
1/2 cup buttermilk
1 teaspoon baking soda
2 eggs, beaten

1 teaspoon almond extract
1/2 teaspoon salt

CHOCOLATE ICING
1/2 cup (1 stick) butter, softened
1/4 cup baking cocoa
2/3 cup evaporated milk
1 (16-ounce) package
  confectioners' sugar
1/2 cup chopped pecans

CAKE
Sift the flour and sugar into a large bowl. Combine the baking cocoa, butter, water and oil in a saucepan. Bring to a boil, stirring frequently. Pour over the dry ingredients and mix well. Mix the buttermilk and baking soda in a bowl. Add to the batter and mix well. Add the eggs, almond extract and salt and mix well. Pour into a greased and floured 9×13-inch baking pan. Bake in a preheated 400-degree oven for 18 minutes or until the cake tests done. Remove to a wire rack and immediately spread the icing over the hot cake. Let cool before serving.

ICING
Beat the butter, baking cocoa, evaporated milk and confectioners' sugar in a mixing bowl until smooth. Stir in the pecans.

When making chocolate cake, use cocoa instead of flour to coat your cake pan. This will keep the cake from having white-flour "dust" on it when you remove it from the pan.

To keep your hands clean while greasing a baking pan, place your hand in side a plastic sandwich bag before dipping it into the can of shortening. The pliable bag greases the surface more easily than a piece of waxed paper.

CHOCOLATE KAHLÚA CAKE

SERVES 12 TO 14

1 (2-layer) package chocolate fudge cake mix
2 cups sour cream
2 eggs
$1/2$ cup vegetable oil
$1/4$ cup Kahlúa
$1/4$ cup water
1 (3-ounce) package vanilla instant pudding mix
1 cup (6 ounces) chocolate chips

Combine the cake mix, sour cream, eggs, oil, Kahlúa, water and pudding mix in a bowl and mix until smooth. Stir in the chocolate chips. Pour into a greased bundt pan. Bake in a preheated 350-degree oven for 50 minutes or until the cake tests done. Cool in the pan for 30 minutes. Invert onto a serving plate and serve warm.

C'est bon

That's good!

DREAMY COCONUT CAKE

SERVES 12

1 (2-layer) package white cake mix
1 1/3 cups water
1/3 cup vegetable oil
3 eggs
1 can cream of coconut
8 ounces cream cheese, softened
1/4 cup milk
1/2 cup confectioners' sugar
1 tablespoon vanilla extract
1/2 cup flaked coconut
1 (12-ounce) container frozen whipped
topping, thawed
1/2 cup flaked coconut
1/4 cup flaked coconut

Combine the cake mix, water, oil and eggs in a mixing bowl and beat for 2 minutes. Pour into a greased and floured 9×13-inch baking pan and bake according to the package directions. Remove to a wire rack and poke holes over the top of the hot cake with a wooden spoon handle. Pour the cream of coconut evenly over the cake. Let stand until cool. Beat the cream cheese in a mixing bowl until smooth. Beat in the milk, confectioners' sugar and vanilla. Fold in 1/2 cup flaked coconut and whipped topping. Sprinkle 1/2 cup flaked coconut over the top of the cooled cake. Cut the cake in half and remove one-half to a serving plate. Spread one-third of the cream cheese mixture over the top of the cake on the serving plate. Top with the remaining cake half. Spread the remaining cream cheese mixture over the top and sides of the cake. Sprinkle with 1/4 cup flaked coconut. Chill, covered, overnight.

Cream of coconut may be found in the baking aisle or mixed drinks aisle at the grocery store. You may use three-fourths can unsweetened coconut milk mixed with one (14-ounce) can sweetened condensed milk instead of the cream of coconut.

Make ahead

Desserts • 187

KEY LIME CAKE

SERVES 16 TO 20

CAJUN TWO-STEP

*Cajun Two-Step is a folk dance
in which partners dance to fast
music with a 4/4 beat. The term
two-step is also applied to the
up-tempo songs that accompany
these dance-steps. Traditionally,
couples move in a counter-
clockwise direction around the
floor, with the gentleman moving
forward and the lady backward.
The basic movement is step left,
step together, step left, touch, step
right, touch.*

KEY LIME CAKE
1 (2-layer) package lemon cake mix
1 (3-ounce) package lime gelatin
1 1/2 cups vegetable oil
5 eggs
1/2 cup orange juice
1/4 cup confectioners' sugar
1/2 cup Key lime juice

CREAM CHEESE ICING
8 ounces cream cheese, softened
1/2 cup (1 stick) butter, softened
1 teaspoon vanilla extract
1 (16-ounce) package confectioners' sugar
less 1/4 cup (used for cake)

CAKE
Combine the cake mix, gelatin, oil, eggs and orange juice in a mixing bowl.
Beat at medium speed for 3 minutes. Pour into three greased and floured 8- or
9-inch cake pans. Bake in a preheated 350-degree oven for 25 minutes or until
the cakes test done. Cool in the pans for 10 minutes. Remove to a wire rack.
Combine the confectioners' sugar and Key lime juice in a bowl and mix well.
Spread over the warm cake layers and let cool completely.

ICING
Beat the cream cheese and butter in a mixing bowl. Beat in the vanilla and
confectioners' sugar until smooth. Spread between the layers and over the
top and side of the cooled cake.

BUTTERMILK FIG CAKE

SERVES 12

BUTTERMILK FIG CAKE	2 cups figs, chopped
2 cups all-purpose flour	1 cup chopped pecans
1 1/2 cups sugar	
1 teaspoon salt	BUTTERMILK SAUCE
1 teaspoon baking soda	1 cup sugar
1/2 teaspoon baking powder	1/2 cup (1 stick) butter
1/2 cup vegetable oil	1/2 cup buttermilk
3 eggs	1 tablespoon corn syrup
1 cup buttermilk	1 tablespoon vanilla extract
1 tablespoon vanilla extract	1/2 teaspoon baking soda

CAKE

Combine the flour, sugar, salt, baking soda and baking powder in a large bowl and mix well. Add the oil, eggs, buttermilk, vanilla, figs and pecans and mix well. Pour into a greased and floured bundt pan. Bake in a preheated 350-degree oven for 45 minutes or until the cake tests done. Cool in the pan for 10 minutes. Remove to a wire rack and poke holes over the cake with a fork or wooden pick.

SAUCE

Combine the sugar, butter, buttermilk, corn syrup, vanilla and baking soda in a saucepan. Bring to a simmer, stirring frequently. Cook for 3 minutes, stirring occasionally. Pour over the cake.

You may bake this cake in a greased and floured 9×13-inch baking pan and pour the sauce directly over the cake.

Krewe

a private social club that sponsors balls, parades, and other festivities as part of the Mardi Gras celebration

TROPICAL PARADISE CAKE

SERVES 12 TO 15

CAKE
3 cups all-purpose flour
2 cups sugar
1 teaspoon salt
1 teaspoon baking soda
1 1/2 cups vegetable oil
3 eggs, beaten
1 1/2 cups pecan halves, chopped
4 very ripe bananas, thinly sliced
1 (8-ounce) can crushed pineapple, drained
1 teaspoon vanilla extract

CREAM CHEESE FROSTING
16 ounces cream cheese, softened
1 cup (2 sticks) margarine, softened
2 (1-pound) packages confectioners' sugar
2 teaspoons vanilla extract
1/2 cup pecan halves, chopped

CAKE
Combine the flour, sugar, salt and baking soda in a bowl and mix well. Add the oil and eggs and stir just until moistened. Do not beat. Gently stir in the pecans, bananas, pineapple and vanilla; the batter will be thick.

Spread the batter evenly in three greased and floured 8-inch cake pans. Bake in a preheated 350-degree oven for 25 to 30 minutes or until a wooden pick inserted in the centers comes out clean. Cool in the pans for 10 minutes and remove to a wire rack to cool completely.

CREAM CHEESE FROSTING
Beat the cream cheese and margarine in a mixing bowl until creamy. Add the confectioners' sugar and vanilla and beat until of a spreading consistency. Spread a generous amount of the frosting between the layers and then spread the remaining frosting over the top and side of the cake. Sprinkle with the pecans. Store in the refrigerator.

MARDI GRAS KING CAKE
SERVES 24

1 1/4 cups milk
1/4 cup (1/2 stick) chilled butter, cut into slices
1/4 cup granulated sugar
1 teaspoon salt
1 heaping tablespoon dry yeast
1 egg, beaten
4 1/2 cups all-purpose flour
Melted butter

Cinnamon-sugar
1-inch plastic or ceramic baby doll
2 cups confectioners' sugar
2 tablespoons milk or cream
1/8 teaspoon almond extract or lemon juice
Purple, green, and yellow colored sugars

Scald the milk in a glass 2-cup measuring cup in the microwave. Add 1/4 cup butter, granulated sugar, and salt and stir until the sugar is dissolved and the butter is melted. Let cool slightly and stir in the yeast. Add the egg and stir well with a fork. Add the yeast mixture to the flour in a bowl and mix well. Knead the dough on a floured work surface. Shape the dough into a ball and place in a buttered bowl and brush with melted butter. Cover with a damp kitchen towel and let rise in a warm place until doubled in bulk.

Punch down the dough. Roll out the dough on a floured work surface to a long rectangle. Brush with generously with melted butter and sprinkle with cinnamon-sugar. Roll as for a jelly roll, sealing the edges and ends, and shape into a circle or oval. Place seam side down on a foil-covered baking sheet coated with nonstick cooking spray. Secure the ends of the roll together with wooden picks and brush with melted butter. Let rise in a warm place for 30 to 45 minutes.

Bake in a preheated 375-degree oven for 15 to 20 minutes, covering loosely with foil if becoming too brown. Let cool slightly and press the doll into the underside of the cake. Combine the confectioners' sugar, milk and almond extract in a bowl and mix well. Drizzle the glaze over the top of the cake and sprinkle with colored sugars.

You may use 1/2 to 3/4 cup packed brown sugar plus chopped pecans or sweetened, softened cream cheese instead of the cinnamon-sugar.

You may make the dough in a bread machine, following manufacturer's directions.

KING CAKE

The King Cake, a Mardi Gras tradition, originated in France in the 12th century to honor the three Kings and their visit to the baby Jesus. It is an oval, sugary pastry that has a tiny plastic doll hidden inside. Tradition dictates that whoever finds the doll is crowned "King" (or Queen) and is expected to carry on the carnival festivities by hosting the next King Cake party. The colors of the cake, which are the colors of Mardi Gras, each have a meaning; purple stands for justice, green represents faith, and gold symbolizes power.

PISTACHIO NUT SWIRL CAKE

SERVES 16

1 (2-layer) package yellow
cake mix
1 (3-ounce) package pistachio
instant pudding mix
4 eggs
1 cup sour cream

¹/₂ cup vegetable oil
¹/₂ teaspoon almond extract
¹/₂ cup sugar
¹/₂ cup chopped pecans
1 teaspoon cinnamon

Combine the cake mix, pudding mix, eggs, sour cream, oil and almond extract in a mixing bowl and beat at medium speed for 2 minutes. Combine the sugar, pecans and cinnamon in a bowl and mix well. Pour one-third of the batter into a bundt pan coated with nonstick cooking spray and sprinkle with half the nut mixture. Top with one-third of the batter and sprinkle with the remaining nut mixture. Top with the remaining batter. Bake in a preheated 350-degree oven for 50 minutes or until the cake tests done. Cool in the pan for 15 minutes. Remove to a wire rack to cool completely.

FAVORITE POUND CAKE

SERVES 16

3 cups all-purpose flour
1 teaspoon salt
1 cup buttermilk
¹/₄ teaspoon baking soda
1 cup (2 sticks) butter, softened

3 cups sugar
4 eggs
2 teaspoons almond extract
1 teaspoon vanilla extract

Pound cake received its name because originally the recipe required one pound each of the following ingredients: flour, butter, eggs, and sugar.

Combine the flour and salt and mix well. Mix the buttermilk and baking soda in a small bowl.

Beat the butter and sugar in a mixing bowl until light and fluffy. Add the eggs, one at a time, beating well after each addition. Stir in the dry ingredients alternately with the buttermilk mixture; do not overmix. Stir in the almond extract and vanilla. Pour into a greased and floured bundt pan. Bake in a preheated 350-degree oven for 1 hour or until the cake tests done. Cool in the pan for 10 minutes. Remove to a wire rack to cool completely.

Serve with fresh Louisiana strawberries and whipped cream for an incredible strawberry shortcake.

WALNUT RUM SPICE CAKE

SERVES 25 TO 30

1 (2-layer) package spice cake mix
4 eggs
1 1/3 cups buttermilk
1/3 cup vegetable oil
1/2 cup packed brown sugar
1 1/2 cups chopped walnuts, toasted
1 cup rum
1 cup granulated sugar
1/4 cup (1/2 stick) butter

Combine the cake mix, eggs, buttermilk, oil and brown sugar in a mixing bowl.
Beat at low speed until moistened and then at medium speed for 2 minutes.
Stir in the walnuts. Pour into a greased and floured 12-cup bundt pan. Bake in
a preheated 325-degree oven for 50 to 55 minutes or until a wooden pick
inserted in the center comes out clean. Cool in the pan for 10 minutes. Poke
holes over the cake with a wooden pick. Combine the rum, granulated sugar
and butter in a saucepan. Bring to a simmer and cook for 2 minutes, stirring
frequently. Spoon over the hot cake and let the cake cool for 2 hours before
inverting onto a serving plate.

Gâteau
a French word for cake

CHOCOLATE CRINKLES

MAKES 6 DOZEN

4 ounces unsweetened chocolate, melted
1/2 cup vegetable oil
2 cups granulated sugar
4 eggs
2 teaspoons vanilla extract
2 cups all-purpose flour
2 teaspoons baking powder
1/2 teaspoon salt
1 cup confectioners' sugar

Combine the melted chocolate, oil and granulated sugar in a bowl and mix well. Add the eggs, one at a time, stirring well after each addition. Stir in the vanilla. Add the flour, baking powder and salt and mix well. Chill for several hours to overnight. Drop teaspoonfuls of dough into the confectioners' sugar and roll to coat. Shape into balls and place 2 inches apart on a greased baking sheet. Bake in a preheated 350-degree oven for 10 to 12 minutes; do not overbake. Remove the cookies to a wire rack to cool.

Make ahead

CHOCOLATE OATMEAL COOKIES

MAKES 2 DOZEN

2 cups sugar
3 tablespoons baking cocoa
1/2 cup (1 stick) butter or margarine
1/2 cup milk, or 2/3 cup evaporated milk
1 1/2 tablespoons peanut butter (optional)
3 cups quick-cooking oats
1 teaspoon vanilla extract
1 cup chopped pecans (optional)

Combine the sugar, baking cocoa, butter, milk and peanut butter in a saucepan. Bring to a boil and cook for 3 minutes, stirring frequently. Remove from the heat. Add the oats, vanilla and pecans and mix well. Drop by spoonfuls onto waxed paper and let cool.

Swamp Pop is a style of music created by Cajun and Creole musicians in the late 1950s. It is a hybrid of pop, rock, and rhythm and blues. Accordions and French lyrics are rare in swamp pop, which features typical R&B instrumentation and a distinct regional identity coming from a soulful, emotional vocal style that has strong connections with zydeco and Cajun music.

Whenever you need just a bit of chocolate for sauces, ganache, or a quick topping, try using a grater (large holes work best). Hold the chocolate by the wrapper to keep it from melting. To store, seal the grated chocolate in a plastic bag and keep in a cool, dark place—not the refrigerator or freezer.

BUTTON COOKIES

MAKES 2 TO 3 DOZEN COOKIES

2 cups all-purpose flour
1 teaspoon baking soda
1/4 teaspoon ginger
1/4 teaspoon ground cinnamon
1/4 teaspoon salt
1 cup packed brown sugar
3/4 cup (1 1/2 sticks) butter
1 egg
1 cup chopped nuts
1 teaspoon vanilla extract
Granulated sugar for coating

Sift the flour, baking soda, ginger, cinnamon and salt together. Cream the brown sugar and butter in a mixing bowl. Beat in the egg until blended. Add the dry ingredients and beat until smooth. Fold in the nuts and vanilla. Chill the dough for several hours.

Shape the dough into balls and coat with granulated sugar. Place the balls 2 inches apart on a buttered cookie sheet and flatten with a fork. Bake in a preheated 375-degree oven for 8 to 10 minutes or until light brown. Cool on the cookie sheet for 2 minutes and remove to a wire rack to cool completely. Store in an airtight container.

GRAHAM CRACKER COOKIES

MAKES 2 TO 3 DOZEN COOKIES

Graham crackers
1 cup packed light brown sugar
1 cup (2 sticks) butter
1 cup chopped pecans

Line a cookie sheet with graham crackers; make sure the edges of the graham crackers touch. Combine the brown sugar, butter and pecans in a saucepan and bring to a boil. Boil for 3 minutes, stirring occasionally.

Pour the caramel mixture evenly over the graham crackers and bake in a preheated 350-degree oven for 10 minutes. Immediately remove the cookies to a wire rack to cool.

BROWNIE MALLOW BARS

MAKES 2 TO 3 DOZEN

1 (family-size) package fudge
brownie mix
1 (10-ounce) package
miniature marshmallows

2 cups (12 ounces)
chocolate chips
1 cup peanut butter
1 tablespoon butter
1 1/2 cups crisp rice cereal

Prepare the brownie mix according to the package directions. Pour into a 9×13-inch baking pan coated with nonstick cooking spray. Bake in a preheated 350-degree oven for 28 to 30 minutes. Sprinkle the marshmallows over the hot brownies and bake for 3 minutes longer. Remove to a wire rack to cool.

Cook the chocolate chips, peanut butter and butter in a saucepan over low heat until melted and smooth, stirring constantly. Remove from the heat and stir in the cereal. Spread over the marshmallow layer in the pan. Chill for 1 to 2 hours or until firm before cutting.

OOEY-GOOEY CARAMEL BROWNIES

MAKES 18 TO 24 BROWNIES

1 (14-ounce) can sweetened
condensed milk
1 (2-layer) package devil's food
cake mix
1/2 cup (1 stick) butter, melted

1 (9-ounce) package caramels
1/2 cup (3 ounces) semisweet
chocolate chips
Confectioners' sugar (optional)

Coat a 9×13-inch baking pan with nonstick cooking spray and dust lightly with flour. Reserve 1/3 cup of the condensed milk. Combine the remaining condensed milk, cake mix and butter in a bowl and mix well. Pat half the cake mix mixture over the bottom of the prepared cake pan and bake in a preheated 350-degree oven for 10 minutes.

Combine the reserved 1/3 cup condensed milk and the caramels in a double boiler or in a microwave-safe dish and cook or microwave until blended, stirring occasionally.

Sprinkle the chocolate chips over the hot baked layer and drizzle with the caramel mixture. Crumble the remaining cake mix mixture over the top and bake for 15 to 20 minutes longer. Cool in the pan on a wire rack. Dust with confectioners' sugar and cut into bars. Use fat-free sweetened condensed milk, if desired.

CRÈME DE MENTHE BARS
MAKES 5 DOZEN

CHOCOLATE BARS
4 ounces unsweetened chocolate
1 cup (2 sticks) margarine
4 eggs
2 cups sugar
1 cup sifted all-purpose flour
1/2 teaspoon salt
1 teaspoon vanilla

CRÈME DE MENTHE FILLING
1/2 cup (1 stick)
   margarine, softened
4 cups confectioners' sugar
1/4 cup cream
1/4 cup crème de menthe

CHOCOLATE TOPPING
1 cup (6 ounces) chocolate chips
1/4 cup (1/2 stick) margarine
3 tablespoons water

BARS
Combine the chocolate and margarine in the top of a double boiler over hot water. Cook until the mixture is melted, stirring occasionally. Remove the top of the double boiler from the water and let cool slightly. Beat the eggs in a mixing bowl until light and frothy. Beat in the sugar gradually. Add the flour, salt, vanilla and melted chocolate mixture and beat for 1 minute. Pour into a greased 9×13-inch baking pan. Bake in a preheated 350-degree oven for 25 minutes; do not overbake. Remove to a wire rack to cool completely.

FILLING
Beat the margarine and confectioners' sugar in a mixing bowl and gradually beat in the cream and crème de menthe. Beat until light and fluffy. Spread over the cooled bar layer. Chill until firm.

TOPPING
Combine the chocolate chips, margarine and water in the top of a double boiler over hot water. Cook until the mixture is melted, stirring occasionally. Drizzle over the filling and swirl with a wooden pick. Chill until firm.

   You may prepare and bake a package of brownie mix according to the package directions instead of making the bar layer.

Praline Pecan Bites

MAKES 1 1/2 DOZEN

1 cup packed brown sugar
1/2 cup bread flour
10 2/3 tablespoons (2/3 cup) butter, softened
2 eggs, beaten
1/2 cup pecans, chopped

Mix the brown sugar and flour together. Combine the butter, eggs and pecans in a bowl and mix well. Add the flour mixture stir just until blended. Fill miniature muffin cups coated with nonstick cooking spray two-thirds full. Bake in a preheated 350-degree oven for 15 minutes. Remove to a wire rack to cool.

Praline

A Louisiana blending of brown sugar, butter, and our finest pecans

GENTLEMAN'S BOURBON BALLS

MAKES 3 DOZEN

1 cup crushed vanilla wafers	2 tablespoons light corn syrup
1 cup confectioners' sugar	1/4 cup (or less) bourbon or rum
2 tablespoons baking cocoa	1/2 cup granulated sugar
1 cup (or more) chopped pecans	Pecan halves

Combine the crushed wafers, confectioners' sugar, baking cocoa and pecans in a bowl and mix well. Add the corn syrup and bourbon and mix well. Shape into small balls and coat in the granulated sugar. Place one pecan half on each ball and press gently.

Silpat is a liner made of silicone and fiberglass which replaces the need for parchment paper. The nonstick surface allows baked goods to slide off the mat after baking without the need for a spatula.

CHOCOLATE KISSES

MAKES 4 TO 5 DOZEN

3 egg whites	1/2 teaspoon vanilla extract
1/2 teaspoon cream of tartar	1 cup (or more) pecans,
1 cup superfine sugar	coarsely chopped, or
3 tablespoons baking cocoa, sifted	1/2 cup flaked coconut

Beat the egg whites in a mixing bowl until foamy. Add the cream of tartar and beat until soft peaks form. Beat in the sugar and baking cocoa 1 tablespoon at a time. Fold in the vanilla and pecans. Drop by teaspoonfuls onto a Silpat-lined cookie sheet. Place in a preheated 450-degree oven and turn off the heat. Leave in the oven for at least 8 hours without opening the oven door.

If using flaked coconut instead of pecans, slightly reduce the amount of sugar.

Make these cookies on a day with low humidity or they may become chewy.

Make ahead

Seven or eight egg whites equal 1 cup. You can freeze and re-freeze egg whites.

ALMOND BUTTER TOFFEE

MAKES ABOUT 1 1/2 POUNDS

12 ounces slivered almonds (about 2 3/4 cups)
1 cup (2 sticks) butter
1 cup sugar
6 tablespoons light corn syrup
2 tablespoons water
2 cups (12 ounces) semisweet chocolate chips

Spread the almonds over a shallow baking pan. Toast in a preheated 350-degree oven for 10 minutes or until golden brown. Reserve 1/2 cup of the almonds and finely chop.

Combine the butter, sugar, corn syrup and water in a saucepan and bring to a boil, stirring constantly. Cook to 290 degrees on a candy thermometer, hard-crack stage, stirring constantly. Stir in the remaining 2 1/4 cups almonds quickly. Pour onto a foil-lined baking sheet and spread quickly. Sprinkle with the chocolate chips and let stand for 3 minutes.

Spread the melted chocolate over the toffee. Sprinkle with the reserved almonds and press gently into the chocolate. Chill until firm. Break into pieces. Store in an airtight container in the refrigerator.

Gris Gris

good luck charm typically made as small cloth
bags containing personal items used to attract money
or love, guard the home, maintain good health,
or ward off evil and protect the owner.

TOASTED PECAN CLUSTERS
SERVES 40

6 tablespoons butter
6 cups pecan pieces
1 (24-ounce) package chocolate candy coating,
chocolate bark or white chocolate almond bark

Melt the butter in a 10×15-inch baking pan in the oven. Add the pecans and stir
to coat. Spread the pecans over the baking pan. Bake in a preheated 300-degree
oven for 30 minutes, stirring every 10 minutes. Melt the candy coating in a
heavy saucepan over low heat. Remove from the heat and let cool for 2 minutes.
Stir in the pecans. Drop by rounded teaspoonfuls onto waxed paper and let cool.
Store in an airtight container in the refrigerator.

Make ahead

ZAPPED PEANUT BRITTLE
MAKES ABOUT 1 1/2 POUNDS

1/2 cup corn syrup
1 cup sugar
1/4 teaspoon salt
2 cups unsalted peanuts
1 tablespoon butter
1 teaspoon vanilla extract
1 teaspoon baking soda

Combine the corn syrup, sugar, salt and peanuts in a microwave-safe bowl and
mix well. Microwave on High for 7 minutes, stirring three or four times. Stir in
the butter and vanilla. Microwave on High for 2 minutes, stirring once. Stir in
the baking soda. Pour onto a baking sheet coated with nonstick cooking spray
and spread quickly. Let cool and break into pieces.

On a humid day, cook candy
to a temperature a degree or so
higher than the recipe indicates.
To prevent crystallization or
grainy candy, sugar must
dissolve completely over low
heat; stir down any grains
from side of saucepan. After the
candy has boiled, do not stir
until it has cooled as the recipe
indicates. To prevent crystals,
do not scrape pan or stir candy
during cooling.

COWBOY CANDY

SERVES 24

12 whole honey or chocolate graham crackers
6 squares white almond bark
$1/2$ cup creamy peanut butter
2 squares chocolate almond bark
2 squares white almond bark

Line a 10×15-inch pan with foil and coat with nonstick cooking spray. Fit the graham crackers in a single layer into the prepared pan. Combine 6 squares white almond bark and the peanut butter in a microwave-safe bowl. Microwave on High until melted, stirring occasionally. Spread over the graham crackers.

Melt the chocolate almond bark in a microwave-safe bowl in the microwave and drizzle over the white almond bark layer. Melt 2 squares white almond bark in a microwave-safe bowl in the microwave. Drizzle over the chocolate almond bark layer and swirl with a wooden pick, if desired. Chill for 10 minutes or until firm. Break into pieces and store in an airtight container in the refrigerator.

Make ahead

Laissez les bon temps roulé

In Southwest Louisiana, it's our way of life,
we "let the good times roll!"

CHOCOLATE TOFFEE CRUNCH

MAKES 6 TO 7 DOZEN PIECES

Regular or low-sodium saltine crackers
1 cup (2 sticks) butter or margarine
1 cup sugar
2 cups (12 ounces) chocolate chips
2 cups (12 ounces) peanut butter chips
Dry-roasted peanuts, whole, coarsely chopped or
finely chopped (optional)

Fit the crackers in a single layer in a foil-lined 10×15-inch baking pan or
coat the pan with nonstick cooking spray. Combine the butter and sugar in
a saucepan. Bring to a boil, stirring frequently. Boil for 3 minutes, stirring
occasionally. Pour evenly over the crackers. Bake in a preheated 400-degree
oven for 5 to 6 minutes. Remove from the oven and turn off the heat.

Sprinkle the chocolate chips and peanut butter chips evenly over the toffee
layer. Return to the oven for 5 minutes. Spread the melted chocolate and
peanut butter chips evenly over the toffee layer and sprinkle with the peanuts.
Return to the oven for 5 minutes. Remove to a wire rack and let cool. Chill for
2 hours. Break into pieces and store in an airtight container in the refrigerator.

Make ahead

LA-LA

*La-La is a name given to Creole
French music and dances before
the term "Zydeco" became
prevalent in the 1960s. Today,
la-la, although rarely used, refers
to old-time Creole French music.*

PEPPERMINT BARK

SERVES 15

8 to 12 large candy canes or 24 small candy canes
1 package almond bark
2 teaspoons peppermint extract

Place the candy canes in a plastic bag and break into pieces with a wooden mallet. Melt the almond bark in a microwave-safe bowl in the microwave. Stir in the peppermint extract. Pour into a foil-lined 10×15-inch pan and spread quickly. Sprinkle with the crushed candy canes. Chill for 10 minutes or until firm. Break into pieces and store in an airtight container in the refrigerator.

CHOCOLATE PARTY MIX

SERVES 16

2 cups (12 ounces) chocolate chips
1 cup peanut butter
1/2 cup (1 stick) butter
1 (17-ounce) box Crispix cereal
1 (16-ounce) package confectioners' sugar

Melt the chocolate chips, peanut butter and butter in a microwave-safe bowl in the microwave, stirring occasionally. Pour over the cereal in a large bowl and mix gently. Add the cereal mixture to the confectioners' sugar in a sealable plastic bag in batches and shake to coat. Remove the coated party mix from the bag, shaking off any excess confectioners' sugar. Store in an airtight container or sealable plastic bag.

Oops — I thought I had that!

Baking powder—1 teaspoon (double acting)	1/4 teaspoon baking soda plus 5/8 teaspoon cream of tartar
Bread crumbs—1 cup	3/4 cup cracker crumbs (dry)
Brown sugar, light—1 cup	1/2 cup dark brown sugar plus 1/2 cup granulated sugar
Butter —1 cup (2 sticks; 16 tablespoons)	7/8 cup vegetable oil, lard or vegetable shortening
Buttermilk—1cup	1 3/4 teaspoons cream of tartar plus 1 cup milk OR 1 tablespoon vinegar or lemon juice plus enough milk to equal 1 cup (let stand for 5 minues)
Confectioners' sugar—1 cup	1/2 cup plus 1 tablespoon granulated sugar
Cornstarch—1 tablespoon	2 tablespoons all-purpose flour OR 2 teaspoons arrowroot
Cracker crumbs—1 cup	1 1/4 cups bread crumbs
Flour—2 tablespoons all-purpose (for thickening)	1 tablespoon cornstarch OR 4 teaspoons arrowroot OR 2 tablespoons quick-cooking tapioca
Garlic—1 small clove	1/8 teaspoon garlic powder
Ginger (fresh)—1 tablespoon	1/8 teaspoon powdered ginger
Granulated sugar—1 cup	1 3/4 cups confectioners' sugar OR 1 cup packed light brown sugar
Half-and-half cream—1 cup	1 1/2 tablespoons butter plus enough whole milk to equal 1 cup
Honey—1 cup	1 1/4 cups granulated sugar plus 1/4 cup of any other liquid used in recipe
Lemon juice—1 teaspoon	1/2 teaspoon vinegar
Mustard, prepared—1 tablespoon	1 teaspoon powdered mustard
Sour cream—1 cup	1 tablespoon lemon juice plus enough evaporated whole milk to equal 1 cup OR 3/4 cup buttermilk or plain yogurt plus 1/3 cup butter
Tomato juice—1 cup	1/2 cup tomato sauce plus 1/2 cup water
Tomato sauce—1 cup	3/8 cup tomato paste plus 1/2 cup water
Vinegar—1 teaspoon	2 teaspoons lemon juice
Whipping cream—1 cup	3/4 cup whole milk plus 1/3 cup butter
Whole milk—1 cup	1 cup nonfat (skim) milk plus 2 tablespoons butter OR 1/2 cup evaporated whole milk plus 1/2 cup water
Yogurt—1 cup	1 cup buttermilk OR 1 cup milk plus 1 tablespoon lemon juice

Information obtained from *The New Food Lover's Companion*, 2nd Edition, Sharon Tyler Herbst, Barron's Cooking Guide, Copyright 1995

History of the
Junior League of Lake Charles, Inc.

MISSION

The Junior League of Lake Charles, Inc., is an organization of women committed to promoting voluntarism, developing the potential of women, and improving the community through the effective action and leadership of trained volunteers. Its purpose is exclusively educational and charitable.

The women of the Junior League of Lake Charles, Inc., are a collection of talented and committed community activists who move the earth by day and entertain as graciously as their mothers did when the day is done. In seventy-four years they have shaped the spirit and face of our community through dedication and a commitment to make Southwest Louisiana a better place for their families and their neighbors. Today, five hundred members strong, they continue to do this important work with fortitude and determination.

The history of the Junior League of Lake Charles, Inc., dates back to 1933. The United States faced rampant poverty and thousands of people across the country were both jobless and homeless. In November of that year, eleven young women gathered at the Majestic Hotel, in Lake Charles, Louisiana, simply because they wanted to do something to help their community. They soon invited friends to join them and in 1934 they became the Junior Welfare League. This extraordinary act of compassion and voluntarism changed the face of Lake Charles forever.

In those early days, the financial backbone of the League came from an anonymous donation of $1,000 and profits of $313.56 from the first Charity Ball. Among the League's early projects were Health and TB clinics for preschool children, a Christmas Doll and Toy fund, and Soup Kitchens for indigent children established in the schools.

By 1942, the world was engaged in war and the extremely adaptable Junior Welfare League established five casualty stations, Junior Junction, Teenage Canteen, Emergency Child Welfare, and Emergency Aid to Indigent Families.

After thirty-four years as an effective organization, the Junior Welfare League was honored to become the 212th member of the Association of Junior Leagues.

Proud of our involvement in the community, the Junior League of Lake Charles, Inc., has served as a catalyst for the creation of many projects including the ones listed below:

Arts & Humanities Council of
Southwest Louisiana Arts Fest
Calcasieu Community Clinic
The Children's Museum
Christmas in April
Court Appointed Special Advocates (CASA)
Family and Youth Counseling Agency
First Steps
Harbour House
Heritage Awareness/Heritage Hike
Heritage Gallery
Imperial Calcasieu Museum

Kids Choice Puppets
Lake Charles Symphony
Liberty Belles
Literacy Council of Southwest Louisiana
Mistletoe and Moss
Nearly New Shop
Pirate's Pantry Cookbook
Prevent Child Abuse Louisiana (PCAL)
Speech and Hearing Center
Substance Abuse Resource Center
Teen Leadership Council (TLC)
Volunteer Center of Southwest Louisiana

Our logo, a majestic oak tree, its roots firmly planted and its branches reaching toward the sky inscribed with, "Serving, Strengthening, Sustaining the Community" continues to inspire us. The eleven founding members would surely be proud of the incredible legacy they have left.

Our vision remains clear as we enthusiastically address the needs of our community, by donating seed money, partnering with community organizations, and providing leadership, volunteers, training, and education for a better tomorrow.

VISION

Our organization works toward a common goal while providing training opportunities for its members. Our vision is to serve the Southwest Louisiana community by strengthening and enriching its families.

Special Acknowledgments

On behalf of the Junior League of Lake Charles, Inc., we extend our heartfelt appreciation to the membership, their families, and friends. This outstanding group of supporters were responsible for the submission of more than eight hundred recipes, countless hours of testing, and generosity beyond our wildest expectations to make this book possible. It definitely "takes a village" to produce a cookbook of this caliber and we are thankful to all those who helped us, especially the following:

Christy Ammons	Gray Plantation
Val Archer	Jenny Leach
Pam Breaux	Elizabeth Martel
Karen and Ken Chamberlain	Victor Monsour
Patricia Duhon	Bill Shaddock
Cassie Gage	Ann and Ray Todd
	Kelli Wimberly

Shirley and Tom Henning

Shively and Gene Lampson

Thank you for allowing us to photograph your beautiful homes for our book.

Thank you, too . . .

Janice Ackley	Charlotte McCann
Acme Rental	Amanda McElveen
Todd Ammons	Susan McElveen
Amber Belaire	Linda Moffett
Jean Bolton	Willie and Ben Mount
Kathy Briggs	Cinda Noble
Laurie Cunningham	Paradise Florist
Tara Demarie	Party Time Store
Ronnie Dingler	Jennifer Popov
Holly Fukumitsu	Janet Postell
Skylar Giardina	Que Pasa Taqueria
Frank Granger	Mavis Raggio
Sara Green	Tricia Rapp
Stefanie Gregory	Susan Reed
Whitney Hanks	Mary Savoy
Imperial Calcasieu Museum	Penny Seneca
Amanda Inzer	Craig Shaddock
Lynley Jones	Stacy Shearman
Joseph's Electric	Vikki Shearman
Sherri Kramer	Laura Smith
Lacassine National Wildlife Refuge with U.S. Fish & Wildlife Service	Spain's Gifts and Gourmet Baskets
	Susan Stone
Claude Leach	Jennifer and Joseph Tassin
Laura and Buddy Leach	Karen Taussig
Louisiana Division of the Arts	Lisa Trouth
Hope Lumpkin	Lisa Verrette
Darren Martel	Aubrey White

Our sincere apologies to anyone who contributed to *Marshes to Mansions*
that we may have inadvertently omitted.

Recipe Contributors

Ann Abernethy

Sheryl Romero Abshire

Janice Stutes Ackley

Gay Morgan Aday

Amy Painter Allen

Marie Savant Allison

Christy Drum Ammons

Eric Anson

Cynthia Arabie

Valerie Grode Archer

Garnett Jane "Janey" Barham

Garnett "Joe" E. Barham, MD

Jane Gibson Barham

Kay Collins Barnett

Ruth Beatty

Amber Holladay Belaire

Jackie Bettinger

Jean Baldwin Bolton

Pat Bordelon

Bartley Bourgeois

Dinah C. Bradford

Pam Breaux

Kathy Leary Briggs

Pat Briggs

Anne Miller Broderick

Carol Ann Brown

Lori Ann Brown

Ann Carl Bruner

Linda Bunch

Susan Bush

Angie Madere Cain

James D. Cain, Jr.

Reneé Cain

Juliet Gorham Carnahan

Mary Jane Carnahan

Donna Carter

Karen Savant Chamberlain

Ken Chamberlain

Joe Champeaux

Rosalie "Poddy"Leveque Champeaux

Tracey Bleich Churchman

Gayle Smith Cline

George T. Cline

John Cole

Anne Collette

Suzanne Walker Crabtree

Laurie Stine Cunningham

Cecile Cutrer

Kendra Cutrer-Diedrich

Linda Arnold Cutrer

Constance Monlezun Darbonne

Jo David

Nora Ann Davis

Kenneth deBlanc

Jenny Delcambre

Wendy Lemasters Delcambre

Tara Bessette Demarie

Robert Dille

Stacy Briggs Dille

Tinnelle Mancuso Dingler

Deborah Comeaux Dixon

Marilyn Doiron

Carrie Bonin Dondis

Wanda Downs

Patricia Leary Duhon

Reggie Duhon

Carolyn Hill Eakin

Madonna Fazzio

Janice Fontana

Keri Forbess-McCorquodale

Sharon Burns Foret

Tootsie Helman Fournet

David R. Frohn

Mary Ward Frohn

Denise Fusilier

Sandra Allen Futrell

Susan "Suzy" Watts Gaar

Carolyn Gage

Cassie Dingler Gage

Jean Gage

Kathleen Conner Gage

Kelley Shaw Gage

Karen Chaney Garber

Edith Gaines Gibson

Annabella Gorham

Judy Green

Stefanie Jenkins Gregory

Dr. Roger Grimball

Suzanne Byler Guillory

Carmen Cormier Hamilton

Sharon Brown Hanchey

Cindy Shaddock Hanks

Whitney Barrilleaux Hanks

Henry "Rock" Hardy

Kathy Haxthausen

Louis Haxthausen

Penny Boelens Haxthausen

Danielle C. Hay

Dana Dingler Hebert

Cyrena Hight

Cleary Yeatman Hinton

Connie Houssiere

Joe Hulgus

Myriam Cecilia Hutchinson

Chef Wade Hyde

Johnathan Ieyoub

Stephy Ieyoub

Amanda Noland Inzer

Diane Gani Jackson

Melody Carter Jackson

Sandy Canik Jones

Karen Drum Katchur

Sarah Ranier Kearney

Nancy Pickens Keating

Terry Kenney
Donna Fort Kestel
Karen Rosaenfeld Kleinman
Yvonne Savoie Kline
Mary Coleman Knapp
Kit Bonin Lalande
Shively Morgan Lampson
Erin Lang
Cindy Laughlin
Jenny Petrie Leach
Geraldine Leary
Dr. Thomas S. Leary
Melanie Carmen LeJeune
Mary Anne Lemasters
Marcela Bonicelli Lemoine
Barbara Jenks Liles
Lela Melson Lofton
Anne Mancer
May Mancuso
Lois Manena
Becky Gage Maples
Elizabeth Todd Martel
Laurie R. McCall
Nadine Newlin McCall
Charlotte Robertson McCann
Glenda Pecorino McCarty
May McCorquodale
Susan Beatty McElveen
Jeanne McGlathery
Kimberly B. McManus
Marilyn McSwain
Nancy LeLaurin Melton
Joyce Reiter Mendelson
Angela Liggo Miller
Karen Mashburn Miller
Patsy Miller
Leslie Stutes Milligan
Susan Milling

Melissa Mixon
Linda Gregory Moffett
Rhonda Perry Monlezun
Willie Landry Mount
Nicole Pederson Mudd
Laura Kaufman Myrick
Sharon Navas
Wendy Dacus Nocilla
Nanette Noland
Michelle Fontenot North
Karen Nyboer
Gay Todd Parke
Rose Mary "Posey" Pauley
Lisa Streva Perry
Brett Peshoff
Susie Petrie
Colleen Smith Phillips
Nancy Pledger
Jena Price
Juliet Tanner Pridemore
Erica Massey Radde
Ginger Fontana Raftery
Sheila Ranier
Susan Howard Reed
Lynne Daughenbaugh Reid
Richard Reid
Anne Coleman Reinauer
David Reinauer
Richman Reinauer
Kathleen "Sissy" Savant Rice
Denise Robinson
Tina Falgout Rue
Marie Ryan
Elizabeth Savant
John E. Savant, Jr.
John E. Savant, Sr.
Mary Watkins Savoy
Pattie Schmidt

Sheila Schultz
Mary Ben Seeger
Penny Ugland Seneca
Craig Gorham Shaddock
William E. Shaddock
Vikki Trouth Shearman
Darlene Smith
Katie Donelson Smith
Leslie Walker Smith
Robert Craft Smith, M.D.
Annette Bland Sole
Betty Scheib Stevens
Roxie Stewart
Susan Watts Stone
Erin Stritzinger
Karen Ashmore Taussig
Josette Thompson
Pam McCullough Thompson
Ann Smith Todd
Cheryl Steele Todd
Ellene Cook Todd
Lisa Mann Todd
Louis Mann Todd, Sr.
Ray A. Todd, Jr.
Ray A. Todd, Sr.
Terry Treadway
Lisa S. Trouth
Judy Ugland
Barbara Perez Unkel
Sissie Fredeman Villaume
Anita Cox Vincent
Susan Daughenbaugh Vincent
Winn Vinson
Frances Paret Walker
Carole Bruchis Wimberly
Kelli Abboud Wimberly
Linda Wimberly
Reneé Champeaux Wood

Kitchen Testers

Janice Stutes Ackley	Susan "Suzy" Watts Gaar	Jacquelyn Morris
Christy Drum Ammons	Jackie Reed Gabb	Charlotte Moss
Kellye Gandy Anderson	Billy Gage	Ben Mount
Janet Crowe Andrus	Cassie Dingler Gage	Willie Landry Mount
Jennifer Shearer Avery	Trisha Ortego Garber	Nicole Mudd
Tararra Babaz	Jennifer Gary-Tassin	Laura Kaufman Myrick
Kay Collins Barnett	Holly Blaylock Gaudet	Gina Lemoine Neck
Shelli Bridges Barrett	Frank Granger	Wendy Nocilla
Susan Strauss Battestin	Sarah Green	Polly Norman
Amber Holladay Belaire	Stefanie Jenkins Gregory	Christi Hebert Nussmeier
Kelly D. Berryhill	Suzanne Byler Guillory	Kristen Istre Orndoff
Jean Baldwin Bolton	Kourtney Istre Haftmann	Carolyn Peshoff
Carol Moore Bray	Whitney Barrilleaux Hanks	Susie Petrie
Pam Breaux	Kathy Vincent Hanudel	Colleen Smith Phillips
Anne Miller Broderick	Emily Benton Harper	Kelly Goos Phillips
Ann Carl Bruner	Tara Hawkins	Erica Massey Radde
Caprice Bush	Dana Dingler Hebert	Jo Lynn Raetzsch
Lesli Caples	Cyrena Hight	Sherry Raggio
Karen Savant Chamberlain	Connie Houssiere	Tricia Byler Rapp
Ken Chamberlain	Ellen Cogswell Ieyoub	Charlotte Roan
Tracey Bleich Churchman	Kara Istre	Tina Falgout Rue
Christy Cloud-Pousson	Christy Papania Jones	Pattie Schmidt
Kris Cochran	Sara McLeod Judson	Penny Ugland Seneca
Anne Collette	Joe Kelty	Vikki Trouth Shearman
Cecile Cutrer	Melissa Thomas Kelty	Leslie Fenet Streeter
Linda Arnold Cutrer	Sherri Shetler Kramer	Karen McIntosh Stubblefield
Peggy Hazel Dees	Carrie Kuehn	Kathryn Elizabeth Tadlock
Wendy Lemasters Delcambre	Rita Karam Laborde	Karen Ashmore Taussig
Tara Bessette Demarie	Jenny Petrie Leach	Pam McCullough Thompson
Monica Papania Devall	Melanie Carmen LeJeune	Ann Smith Todd
Kendra Cutrer Diedrich	Barbara Jenks Liles	Lisa Mann Todd
Tinnelle Mancuso Dingler	Hope Lumpkin	Ray A. Todd, Jr.
Carrie Bonin Dondis	Elizabeth Todd Martel	Catherine Morrison Townsend
Pat Welch Dow	Julie Kinnaird McCall	Jeff Townsend
Ed Ellington	Nadine Newlin McCall	Lisa S. Trouth
Madeline Ellington	Charlotte Robertson McCann	Judy Ugland
Kristie Evans	Amanda Bush McElveen	Lisa Smith Verrette
Kathyrn Filo	Susan Beatty McElveen	Mary Ann Viator
Carol Flanagan	Ashley McMahon	Pattie White
Nancy Holleyman Fontenot	Kim McManus	Keith Wimberly
Keri Forbess-McCorquodale	Mary Plauche McNulty	Kelli Abboud Wimberly
Sharon Burns Foret	Kim Gandy Melton	Rebekah Rasbeary Winters
Holly Williams Fukumitsu	Linda Gregory Moffett	

Index

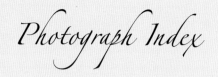

Photograph Index

Cover — A romantic picnic beneath the chandelier's glow at the "knees" of a Cypress tree.

Page 9 — A bathtub, outfitted for a party, in the master bathroom of the Henning home with a beautiful view of Prien Lake.

Pages 22 and 23, clockwise from left to right — a rustic doorknob; cocktails in the foyer of the Lampson home; the Henning's kitchen, a beautiful example of the "heart of the home;" a water hyacinth, which is one of the most productive plants on earth and is known to double in size in two weeks' time; a view from the lake of the Henning home.

Page 37 — A table set for two on the Lampson's Shell Beach Drive wharf overlooking Lake Charles.

Pages 52 and 53, clockwise from left to right — a tugboat escorting a barge down the Intercoastal Waterway, which stretches for more than 2,500 miles around the southern coast of the United States; the Henning boathouse on Prien Lake at sunset; friends spending a summer morning tubing down the river; the sailboat regatta, beneath the I-10 Bridge, on the Calcasieu River; a veil of Spanish moss draped from a tree at the marsh's edge.

Page 69 — An entrée served on the Henning family piano.

Pages 86 and 87, clockwise from left to right — a lake view from the second floor veranda of the Henning home; sunset at the high bridge of Interstate 210. This expanse stretches across Prien Lake and allows vessels to traverse between the Calcasieu River and the Port of Lake Charles; a chandelier suspended at Lorraine Park, which is located at the old wooden bridge across Bayou Lacassine; a long-necked White Ibis, wading in the shallow reflecting waters of the marsh, uses its long curved bill to forage for dinner; an evening skyline of the city of Lake Charles; Calcasieu Parish Courthouse, which was built in 1912 in a renaissance, classical revival style of architecture. In the foreground is a Civil War monument.

Page 105 — A harvest of Louisiana Blue Crabs.

Pages 120 and 121, clockwise from left to right — the delightfully fragrant and extremely popular variety of the water lily with its star-shaped, pure white semi-double flowers with golden yellow stamens; the flight of thousands of Snow Geese as they migrate to the marshes for the winter; a hunter at sunrise, push polling his pirogue to the duck blind; a deserted boathouse floating on the bayou; bass fishing on a beautiful Southwest Louisiana bayou; the birth of an American Alligator. He may have a lifespan of thirty or more years and may grow to be 14 feet long and weigh up to 1,200 pounds; male Mallard Ducks feeding at the surface of the water are known as "dabbling ducks" since they never dive beneath the water, but only tip their heads under to feed. The breeding male is unmistakable with its green head and black backside.

Page 137 — A rice plant at harvest time.

Pages 150 and 151, clockwise from left to right — "man's best friend" patiently waiting for his master's return; braids of garlic, which were historically hung on doors or in the rafters to ward off evil spirits, are today used for decoration and cooking; crab traps stored and ready for their next use; rice being harvested at the Sweet Lake Land & Oil Co., a fourth-generation family farm; shrimp boats, tied up, in Cameron Parish; a young man casting at sunset on Calcasieu Lake.

Page 165 — A featured coconut cake graces the branch of a majestic oak tree at the Lacassine National Wildlife Refuge.

Pages 190 and 191, clockwise from left to right — delicious wild blackberries; wild Louisiana irises and cypress "knees." The iris, which became Louisiana's official wildflower in 1990, grows to a height of 5 to 6 feet. The knees are an extension of the root system of a cypress tree and help brace nearby plants against high winds while also providing oxygen to their submerged roots; a chandelier in the Henning's foyer; local Cajun musicians playing their accordions; Louisiana's state bird, the brown pelican, is on the United States Endangered Species List but appears to be making a strong comeback. It is the only nonwhite pelican in the world and they are famous for the large bill which allows them to scoop salt water into their pouches to seize prey. A 1-month-old pelican will consume an average of 5 pounds of fish per day.

The Junior League of Lake Charles, Inc., is proud to present *Marshes to Mansions*
to you. It follows our very popular and successful cookbook, *Pirate's Pantry*,
which sold more than 100,000 copies. We thank you for supporting our efforts by
purchasing this book. As with our other fund-raising projects,
the success of *Marshes to Mansions* will continue to fund the exciting work of the
Junior League of Lake Charles, Inc., in our community.

To order additional copies of *Marshes to Mansions*, at $28.95
per book plus postage and sales tax, or for more information, please
call us at 337-436-4025, or visit our Web site at www.jllc.net.

Notes

A Creole Good-bye

It is always sad to say good-bye to family

and friends after a get-together,

so we linger on the porch and visit a little more.

As we bid you adieux,

we wish you many grand celebrations and hope that

Marshes to Mansions

becomes a favorite of yours!